SHARED LEADERSHIP DISCIPLINES®

Presented this Jewel to Edo in Singapore
Have joy in sharing your leadership :)
With much blessings always
Best,
[illegible]
29 Aug 2023

PRAISE FOR
SHARED LEADERSHIP DISCIPLINES®

This book is a must read for leaders, team members and coaches all over the world. I have personally experienced sharing leadership with the authors. They have elegantly expressed wisdom through stories from many decades of experience working with global teams. By providing the know-how and roadmap to navigate the complex daily interactions in the workplace, we are inspired to discover the power behind the practice. Let us continue to aspire for, and to sustain a healthy and happy world where people embrace the mindset and practice of shared leadership.

— **Ruby Palma**
LIM Leadership Team, Partner - LIM Philippines,
ICF Philippines Past President

The thought of "shared leadership" first emerged in the early 1920's and much has been written about it since then. As we partner with leaders and teams to create new possibilities, it is not so much the 'What is it about?' and 'Why is it important?' but 'How do I/we implement it?' that we have often been asked. Framing shared leadership with the 5 disciplines and providing simple tools and processes anchored on Action Reflection Learning® has brought shared leadership to life! And this is the excitement that we now experience with leaders and their teams as they use it to unleash their collective wisdom.

— **Maria Teresa Benitez**
LIM Leadership Team, Partner - LIM Philippines

I was introduced to Shared Leadership Disciplines several years ago by LIM. This is a practical strategy in building strong and successful teams who have a shared vision and focused objectives. The journey of building and coaching teams that are facing tough challenges is really fun. And by adopting SLD your outcomes are almost guaranteed.

— **Dr. Ahmed Mostofa**
Chairman and CEO of ARTPharma Pharmaceuticals, Egypt

I have been working with Ernie for more than a decade as a client. The Shared Leadership belief and the 5 SL disciplines have never failed to bring leaders and followers together in a much deeper and meaningful manner. Over the years, we have put too much focus on coaching the leaders but in reality, the leaders and their team members need to be coached together. This will optimize the impact and sustain the change.

— **Andrew Shih**
Former Senior Vice President of HR and Talent Development, MNC Pharma

We have been applying the disciplines of Shared Leadership for over 5 years now. This has resulted in a Highly Aligned Leadership Team, all pulling together in the direction we have ALL determined to deliver the best result for our People, our Country, and our Business. I strongly feel that Shared Leadership will give any organization that added edge to thrive in our very dynamic world.

— **Dr. Beaver R. Tamesis**
President and CEO of Asian Hospital

Shared Leadership is often just a buzzword used by leaders. However, using LIM's techniques and tools, I've seen it as highly effective in building high performing teams in organizations and companies to achieve intended breakthrough results.

— **Chris Tan**
Former Managing Director, MSD Malaysia, Singapore & Indonesia

The principles of Shared Leadership are always a reference point for me in my Leadership journey. Having first worked with Ernie in Asia a decade ago, we crafted a Shared Leadership philosophy and set of principles that elevated the performance of the team I was leading at that time. I've applied a similar approach to the many different teams I've subsequently had the pleasure to lead and would recommend the approach wholeheartedly. Great to see this now in a very readable format for all.

— **Deborah Kobewka**
Chief Executive Officer, Ito World

Being a caring leader with a sustainability mindset is what the world of responsible business needs today. This book provides insights on how such transformation is possible. A must read!

— **Dr. Ekaterina Ivanova**
Associate Professor, Graduate School of Business,
HSE University, Russia

Ernie and Swee Heng provide a better way to lead and coach teams – the shared leadership way. Their insights, extensive practice, easy and practical tools bring out the best in teams who deliver results that matter. This is a must read for anyone who seeks a simple yet profound way to bring to life shared leadership that lasts.

— **Gurbakhish Singh (Gb)**
Shared Leadership Coach, Malaysia / Australia

Ernie and Swee Heng bring their professional experience alive in this book. There are a lot of books on theory of leadership, however, what benefits one most are the ones where the writers have walked the path of practice. Ernie and Swee Heng have put together several years of their coaching experiences with leaders of large and small organizations to make these practical applications available to all who desire a better way to lead and coach.

— **Eugene Cheng**
HR Director, Asia Pacific, Oracle

Shared Leadership is a new concept that Ernie introduced to me and my Finance Leadership Team in an offsite in a very inspiring and pragmatic way. It creates a psychologically safe environment for everybody to take the lead and contribute to our common goal with 100% responsibility for the outcome and success. For me it was a great experience to empower my team and build our vision and culture together.

— **Federica Conci**
CFO Pharmaceutical Diagnostic, GE HealthCare, UK

As a first-time senior team leader getting feedback from team members, I was asked to be a more 'Inspirational Leader'. This was something I could not tangibly conceptualize. 'What is inspirational?' 'What behavior makes an Inspirational Leader?' I was thankful that together with Ernie, my coach at the time, we worked out a strategy to achieve this through developing Shared Leadership. I have been using and expanding on this, utilizing ARL tools to work with successive leadership teams to instill a Shared Leadership culture wherever I went. I consider this a powerful concept that brings immense benefits to the team, as well as to the individual leader. Wherever I go, the notes that I took from workshops on Shared Leadership are always with me.

— **Grace Lau**
Former Managing Director, MSD Hong Kong

Our journey towards organizational transformation started a year back with an acknowledgment of the complexity and the strong existing inherent legacy. To do this alone was ' mission impossible', so we reached out to the experts at LIM who amplified for us the shared leadership philosophy of co-creation and collaboration. The net was cast wide to engage all the functional and organizational leaders across the vast network of 19 hospitals. Everyone's voice was heard. 'HELP' was our mantra — both asking for it and offering it. Not one of us, myself included, can lead alone; we shared the leadership. We are learning as a united family and making a giant leap towards improving the landscape of Filipino Heathcare.

— **Dr Harish Pillai**
CEO, Metro Pacific Health, Philippines

About 3000 years ago, the great philosopher Tao said — The best leadership happens when people don't even know the leader exists. Good leaders seldom speak up yet, everything gets done easily, and the people say, 'It's our natural way.' I think shared leadership is the modern version of Tao's wisdom. By reading this book, you will understand the meaning of shared leadership and you will also learn how to bring shared leadership into your organization, your team, and your personal life.

— **Jane Song**
Managing Director, Song Enterprises, China

This book has captured many heartening stories of team transformations. These stories show the great need of intentional conversations in any organization, so as to drive trust, commitment and accountability. Ernie and Swee Heng had generously shared with their readers the tools they have used for their interventions, transforming teams and conversations across the world. Totally inspirational!

— **Joy Leong**
Senior Manager, People & Organization Development,
Woodlands Health, Singapore

Shared Leadership was a real eye-opening concept for me when I first heard about it from Ernie. Over the past several years, I have seen how it benefited my clients' teams greatly when I introduced it to them. Now it is the key element in my team coaching, team development, and leadership courses.

— **Joyce Chen Kuo-San**
Principal Consultant, Sustainable Leadership Group, China

Through SLD, we cultivated a more open, innovative and inclusive culture. Team ownership resulted in higher organizational engagement. Adopting SLD will create a flexible and a resilient team that will navigate an organization through the VUCA era.

— **Kay Deguchi**
Vice Director, Doya Rehabilitation Clinic, Japan

I am a true believer that being a leader does not mean we must always be the one to stand up to solve issues. Being a leader is about how we can help our people to unlock their potential by allowing them to learn the processes, failing fast and enabling them to be connected, appreciated and be challenged for greater heights. This is true leadership. I thank Ernie and Swee Heng for this Shared Leadership book that really helped me to further sharpen my leadership ability. It gives me more motivation in leading and coaching the younger generations to be their best.

— **Kristina Kristina**

Head of Business Services, Hong Kong & Shanghai Bank, Indonesia

I was first introduced to Ernie and LIM's work in 2000. I have seen first-hand the power of Action Reflection Learning® Principles in creating High Performance Teams and Change Leader Development. This latest book by Ernie and Swee Heng builds on these ARL principles and illustrates clearly the power and impact of applying the 5C's of Shared Leadership Disciplines® to shape and reinforce a high-performance culture within an organization and to better engage hybrid teams, whether remotely or face-to-face.

— **Pam Birkett**

Former VP of the Hong Kong Association of Business & Professional Women, Shared Leadership Coach, Hong Kong

Shared Leadership Disciplines® is a brilliant and carefully laid out roadmap to an obvious, but not always implemented, strategy for success within any group or organization. If you want an involved and motivated workforce, it is essential to build a culture where team members feel valued and listened to. In turn, this will lead to a more engaged and committed team with more and better ideas that will be implemented again and again. In truth, we must heed this invitation to a better way to lead and coach. As a longtime coach who has spent time "in the trenches," I am grateful that Ernie and Swee Heng have taken the time to outline, in exquisite detail, the WHY and the HOW so we can be more impactful leaders and coaches every time.

— **Minx Boren**

Master Certified Coach, USA

This book captures the essence of what leadership should look like in the present day. In a favorable combination of circumstance, time and place, I had the good fortune to learn some of the excellent tools backed by precise concepts detailed in this book. I am now a better person, mother, team member and leader!

— **Dr Rochelle Kinson**
Head of Medical Psychiatry & Senior Consultant,
Woodlands Health, Singapore

Shared Leadership Disciplines® enable leaders to build synergy, commitment and growth in the team. Ultimately it creates a culture of inclusiveness where everyone is engaged and wants to be engaged. I recommend every leader to read, understand and practice the 5 Shared Leadership Disciplines® with the team. A shared leadership team brings happiness to all members and their families.

— **Sivaraman Ambalan**
Founder & CEO, Ikigai Growth Consulting LLP, India

Applying shared leadership within the regional access team allowed us to come together with a common future vision that put the team in the front by instilling accountability among our team with a shared purpose. The "Action Reflection Learning" approach we learned from Ernie enables a learning experience that we continue to use for dialogue and reflection within the team as well as cross functions. Not only has this approach made us a better team from a business performance standpoint, but this journey has also made us a happier team with more personal and caring feelings towards each other.

— **Shay Nahum**
Director of MSD Market Access Europe, Switzerland

The 5Cs - Connect, Contract, Collect, Collaborate and Challenge nicely bring Shared Leadership to life. They have enriched the Shared Leadership concept much beyond a simple rotation of roles or sharing of workload. It is amazing that LIM's tools naturally support these five core disciplines that a Shared Leader must practice as second nature. All the LIM's programs that I participated in or supported have always been packed with a set of powerful yet easy to use tools. These have benefited me in applying them in dealing with my day-to-day business challenges, be it people problems, process problems or tool problems. I am convinced that the same would benefit leaders in many other organizations large and small.

— **Weiguo Wang, Ph.D**
Chief Technology Officer, Create Technologies Pte. Ltd., Singapore. Former Global Head, Transportation, Alcatel-Lucent & EVP, Alcatel Shanghai Bell

Organizational charts often breed the unconscious bias of traditional pyramid leadership. The shared leadership disciplines propounded by Ernie and Swee Heng offer a very impactful approach to build a diversified, well engaged and full ownership leadership team.

— **William Mak**
Former President & APAC CEO of Northern Trust

Since 2018, my organization has recognized the importance of Shared Leadership (also known as Collective Leadership in my organization). The 5 Shared Leadership Disciplines® very succinctly captured the essence of how any leader can effectively enable shared leadership. I've learnt and used many of the tools covered in this book to facilitate team conversations in my organization and seen the results they can deliver. A must-have and practical book for leaders who want to bring out the best of their teams, to operate and thrive in this new and challenging world that we are in. Thanks, Ernie and Swee Heng! This is awesome.

— **Yvonne Ng**
Executive Director, National Healthcare Group College, Singapore

SHARED LEADERSHIP DISCIPLINES®

A Better Way To Lead & Coach

ERNIE TURNER & TAN SWEE HENG

EDITED BY
TONY PEARSON

First published 2023

SHARED LEADERSHIP DISCIPLINES®
A Better Way To Lead & Coach

Author:	Ernie Turner & Tan Swee Heng
Editor:	Tony Pearson
Layout:	Geelyn Lim
Cover design:	Jeraldine Boh
Typeset by:	Candid Creation Publishing LLP 167 Jalan Bukit Merah #05-12 Connection One Tower 4 Singapore 150167
ISBN:	978-981-17258-6-9

To our families
with love, warmth and gratitude

To all our readers, learners and users of this book:
May this book help you
to lead and coach for higher performance,
greater impact and
sustainable outcomes

Contents

Foreword
by Lennart Rohlin

This is a most needed and very timely book! It is about management and leadership; it is also about learning and coaching. It clearly integrates leadership and learning as well as management and coaching.

Much has been written about management and leadership but very seldom with this number of practical concepts and tools to help leaders as well as coaches get things done in real life.

Practical? Yes, and also firmly based on research and work done by scholars and practitioners. Already in the early 1900s Mary Parker Follett wrote "Leadership is not defined by the exercise of power but by the capacity to increase the sense of power among those led".

Most of the ideas behind Shared Leadership are not new. However, Shared Leadership practices generally have not been well understood or clearly defined -- until this book! The processes and practical tools to bring the ideas to life are described with clarity in this book. Ernie and Swee Heng, the authors of this book along with their LIM coaches, have been applying the 5 Shared Leadership Disciplines® effectively with clients around the world.

Shared Leadership Disciplines (SLD®) are also grounded on the concept and practice of Action Reflection Learning (ARL®), developed by LIM and the MiL Institute, a Scandinavian management development institute in the late 1970s. MiL was founded by me and other entrepreneurs, and by Lund University and the business community. Based on new perspectives of both leadership and learning, MiL launched highly appreciated programs for top executives and inspired other universities to develop similar institutes and programs.

As human beings we are committed learners driven by good intentions to create results in cooperation with others for the betterment of the common good – as long as we respect the values of diverse systems, are appreciated with respect and trusted with meaningful responsibilities.

Shared Leadership Disciplines driven by ARL principles are based on how adults naturally learn and develop. These 10 ARL Principles broaden and accelerate this learning process by connecting business transformation to talent development. Participants are stimulated to solve real business challenges as they learn about themselves, their colleagues, teamwork and shared leadership. By reflecting on their experiences, participants develop their own theories for action and learning that transcends the actual situation. The importance of "reflection" explains why Reflection was added to the original Action Learning concept[1].

In the mid 1980s Ernie Turner was invited to MiL by his Swedish partner and MiL member, Lars Cederholm. Shortly thereafter Leadership in International Management (LIM) was founded and Victoria Marsick, a professor from Columbia University, and one of four LIM partners, was invited as "Researcher in Residence" at MiL. For many years Ernie and several of his LIM colleagues took part as staff members in international MiL programs. They made huge contributions to the development of concepts and tools besides making the ARL philosophy known worldwide. LIM members have written several articles and books that further describe where Shared Leadership Disciplines have been applied.

If you are interested in the background and research, begin at the front of this book. If you want to get to the practical concepts and tools as fast as possible then I recommend that you begin with Part 2 and the many practical cases. Here you will find a wealth of experiences, innovative approaches, and powerful insights and conclusions. I was impressed! It is like an exciting novel - storytelling at its best.

We know that diversity of perspectives brings innovation and better decisions to any team. We also know that consensus is needed to get power and action behind strategies. Often diversity of opinion leads to win/lose scenarios. Shared Leadership Disciplines is a way to resolve this dilemma ensuring that every voice is heard.

The Shared Leadership mindset has a much wider importance than being evaluated only in economic business terms. The stakeholder model from the 1980s introduced a wider perspective, but its traditional formulation is not good enough today. Sustainability has to be included from multiple stakeholders' perspectives, especially, from cultural, gender and age perspectives.

We left "The Industrial Society" long ago. During the 1980s and the 1990s, different labels have been developed to characterize what kind of society we are entering: "The Service Society", "The Information Society", "The Knowledge Society", "The Global Society", "The Sustainable Society", "The Tech Society"[2].

I would prefer the concept "The Learning Society". In which I am happy to recommend this book as "required reading".

NB: *Lennart Rohlin was the founder and for 30 years CEO of the Scandinavian Management Development Institute, MiL (1978-2009). Before that he wrote and edited about 20 books on different business topics. He was a professor at Lund University, a Visiting Scholar at Harvard Business School and a professor at Helsinki School of Business. At the same time, he was co-founder and manager of EFL, a foundation for closing the gap between the university and the business community, (1968-78). Lennart Rohlin has also been a free-lance journalist and a world champion fencer. Since 1980 he has owned, developed and managed a group of conference centers as an entrepreneur. Last, but not least, Lennart Rohlin is an opinion leader in the areas of learning while earning, and a mentor and friend to many in LIM.*

[1]Rohlin, Lennart: **Action Reflection Learning** in "Action Learning in Practice", the handbook edited by Mike Pedler. 4th edition 2011. Gower Publishing.

[2]Rohlin, Lennart & Skärvad, Per Hugo & Nilsson, Sven-Åke: **Strategic Leadership in the Learning Society**. 1994/98. MiL Publishers. Studentlitteratur. (In Japanese 1999.)

Preface

This book is a dream come true. It was January 2011, when we began using the two words, Shared Leadership, with Grace Lau, the Managing Director of MSD Hong Kong. Together we defined the concept of Shared Leadership and together with her leadership team we brought these two words to life. Together they created a better place to work, to be and to become. They were more effective, more efficient, more productive as individuals and as a team and together they created a more profitable business. We are forever grateful for the curiosity and courage of Grace and her team in launching a 12-year journey that has transformed so many teams and touched hundreds of lives. Now we have this book to share from what we have learned since then. Thank you, Grace, and your team – especially Andrew Shih and Pam Wong.

Since then, we have advocated Shared Leadership concepts and tools as a better way to lead and coach to all our clients. In the process, we have continued to experiment and share our insights, surprises and discoveries. This book is a record of what we have learned since then. It was only in 2020 that we added the word *Disciplines* to Shared Leadership. It was a deliberate decision and process. Our team spent time naming the 5 Shared Leadership Disciplines® and then identifying the principles, concepts and tools that bring each of these 5 disciplines to life.

This story is still evolving. We, the authors and our community of Shared Leadership Coaches, have been learning, practicing and modeling Shared Leadership Disciplines® in our day-to-day work with our clients as well as within our leadership team, coaching faculty, community of practice and inside any team where we work.

Why did we write this book?

The continuing, substantial changes occurring on our planet are affecting how we live, work and inter-relate. Every country and society are impacted by multiple changes -- social, environmental, technological, political, spiritual, economic and legal. The years that leaders have been battling the pandemic have also created new priorities, challenges and thinking in how to lead organizations and the "awakened" workforce in the post-Covid world where people want more control of their work and life. The message is very clear - we need a better way to lead and coach. Our global economy and the health of our people and our planet requires inclusion, interdependent thinking and collaboration across multiple dimensions.

We are forced to revisit our current leadership paradigms. There have been a host of research studies stating what leaders must consider. Here are just a few of the challenges and opportunities that we will explore in this book: leading hybrid teams; engaging everyone on our team; guaranteeing that every voice is heard; breaking every glass ceiling that exists; leading with transparency and authenticity; welcoming uncertainty as an opportunity to create and innovate; being able to adapt and adopt; being vulnerable and willing to ask for 'HELP'; connecting personally and professionally; constantly challenging the status quo - thinking beyond our business and our country - recognizing that our planet and the people on our planet are our responsibilities too. These are the reasons we are in business anyway. Sustainability and peace are ultimately everyone's business.

The purpose of this book is very simple – we want leaders to be inspired and equipped to share their leadership with their team members and experience the transformation that follows. Meetings become magic. Work becomes meaningful. Team members become engaged. Everyone's voice is heard. The increased sharing of influence, power and ownership by leaders creates an inspiring and inviting environment for team members to speak up, step up and to do more for the team and for each other with a greater sense of purpose. The expression of 'Thank God it's Friday' turns into 'Thank God it's Today'. Every day is a day to look forward to. A day to make a difference.

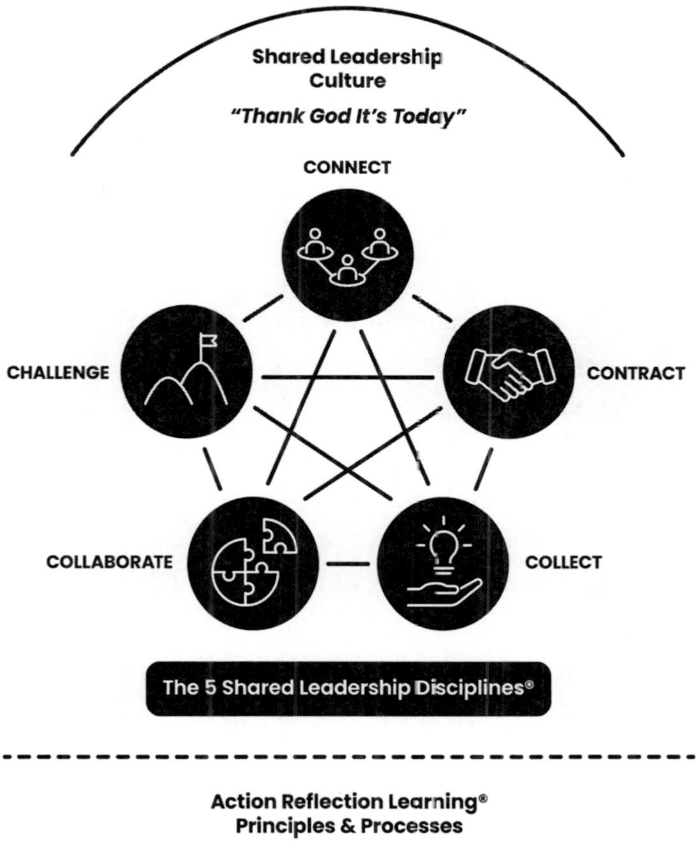

Who is this book for?

This book has been written for every leader, every team member and everyone who is expected to act in the capacity of a 'team coach'. We hope our readers will realize the benefits of sharing their leadership and discover several simple yet practical principles, concepts and tools that they can use to turn their teams into 'shared leadership teams'. We expect the same of team members and those whose role is that of supporting teams in their development and growth.

How is this book organized?

Part One presents the case for Shared Leadership, offers the research, and explains why the current traditional leadership pyramid is broken and needs an alternative.

Part Two provides a detailed description of each of the 5 Shared Leadership Disciplines® including definitions, stories, concepts and practical tools that bring each discipline to life.

Part Three suggests some of the opportunities where the 5 Shared Leadership Disciplines® can be applied in organizations and teams. It includes important insights into how the 5 Disciplines buttress the critical approaches toward inculcating Sustainability into organizational success.

Part Four provides the readers with a clear idea on what it takes to be a Shared Leadership Team Coach.

At the back of the book, we have also shared 15 FAQs that we have encountered over the last several years, 30 Check-In Questions and a summary of the tools that we mentioned in this book. These are intended to be additional resources that our readers can consider using.

Special contributions & acknowledgements

Two other LIM partners have written very important chapters in this book based on their passion and perspective.

Isabel Rimanoczy, a thought leader, and prolific author in her own right, with a life purpose and unstoppable passion to develop a 'sustainability mindset' around the world, has written Chapter 15, *Sustainability — A Strategic Priority*. Leaders and coaches will be inspired by Isabel's mission to collaborate with others to bring this message around the world. We are grateful that she has inspired us to expand our own thinking, sense of purpose and become a part of this global mission.

Willie Anderson, LIM's CEO, and former senior manager from a former Fortune 100 company, has been part of LIM for the last 24 years. Over this time, he has shared in the leadership of LIM and witnessed our transformation as a thought leader in Shared Leadership and Action Reflection Learning®. Willie has written the Afterword of our book where he has shared insights and a vision for our future based on his unique perspective as a savvy businessman, leader of LIM and strong advocate that every voice must be heard.

We are very honored to have Lennart Rohlin, former founder and President of The MiL Institute, our sister company in Sweden, to write our Foreword. Lennart and his organization were the inspiration for the four founding LIM partners, Lars Cederholm, Victoria Marsick, Tony Pearson and Ernie Turner, to bring LIM to life. Over the years Lennart has been our role model and mentor. So, it is with gratitude to you, Lennart, for writing our Foreword and setting the context for our Shared Leadership journey.

Special gratitude goes to Tony Pearson, a founding partner, dear friend, and editor of this book. He has had a front row seat witnessing and leading LIM's twists and turns over our 36-year history as we have all grown up as individuals and as an organization. His attention to the purpose of this book and the content of each page has enabled us as authors to keep our eyes on the message as well as the medium. Thank you, Tony.

We also want to acknowledge the contributions by other members of our Leadership Team, Ruby Palma, Te Benitez and our past leadership team member, Urban Skog. Together with the authors and Willie, they have formed LIM's leadership team. We certainly have fun living, role modeling and enjoying the process and the fruits of sharing our leadership together. We also wish to give a grateful 'Thank You' to Pam Birkett who was so generous in editing various parts of our book.

We would not have been able to complete this book without the support and encouragement of our two life partners, Isabel and Jean. Thank you both!

Last, but not least, we want to give a special shout out to our greater LIM community of Shared Leadership Coaches all over the world. Your active engagement and commitment to meet regularly to learn, share and be actively involved, speaking up and stepping up like the flying geese in the V-formation, is awesome, inspiring and encouraging to both of us. We are thriving because we all share in the leadership. Kudos to all of us!

Our hope for this book

Through this book we hope that more leaders and coaches will embrace the Shared Leadership approach to lead and coach their teams. Many leaders understand, rationally and intuitively, that sharing leadership is the way to lead in our dynamic, complex and chaotic world. What is needed is the tried and tested "know-how" to make Shared Leadership come to life. This book provides that know-how. Now the challenge will be to apply it.

We are at a historic moment. Covid-19 has created seismic shifts in the world of work. The hostilities between Russia and Ukraine have had an impact far beyond their borders. These two events have demonstrated that we, the citizens of this beautiful chaotic world, must learn to collaborate, live and share leadership together. Our people, our society and our planet, deserve no less. The future is in our hands. What will we do?

Part 1

The Case For Shared Leadership

CHAPTER 1

Pyramid Under Attack

"In the fast moving brutally competitive economy, the one thing to be harder than operating with teams is operating without them"

Brian Dumaine
Global Editor, Fortune Magazine

When people think of teams, many picture a single leader at the top of the hierarchy and team members at the base. This is the traditional view of leadership, with a vertical, top-down relationship between the leader and the team members. The leader leads and members follow, and this hierarchical-based leadership forms what is commonly known as the "Traditional Pyramid".

Top-down traditional pyramid

This form of leadership was undoubtedly reinforced by those soldiers returning from World War II, where militaristic leadership behaviors and attitudes of the officer class were necessary. During the 1970s consultants and educators advanced less hierarchical forms of management and leadership, which many companies tried out and adopted. However, many organizations adhered to the top-down model until the 1990s, where the traditional leader atop the pyramid acted as if he knew everything and wanted only compliance from his subordinates. He held the power and authority. He was valued for his functional experiences and skills and paid little attention to developing people skills. He was the boss, he dominated discussions, and usually made the decisions himself.

Since the early 1990s, we witnessed the emergence of major technological, societal, political and cultural change. These affected business, government and not-for-profit worlds alike. Importantly, organizations substantially increased the use of teams—functional, intact, matrix, ad hoc, global, remote, and more recently, hybrid teams. To be effective, team leaders started to make efforts to engage and motivate their teams for higher performance and results. This need for higher employee engagement coincided with, and resulted from, key workplace changes. These included the advent of the Internet, the increasing number of Gen Y and Gen Z (born after 1980 and 1995 respectively) joining and leading the workforce and at the same time, the retirement of Baby Boomers (born 1946 to 1964). There was also the increasing demands for gender equality, inclusivity and diversity, and clear employee expectations that they want their voices be heard.

In our coaching work, we see that many organizations remain more comfortable with the hierarchical structures. This tendency is true in many countries, especially in times of uncertainty. While organizations have become flatter in structure, there is still a clear need for top management to clarify the company mission, develop the business strategy and shape the organizational culture. And to accomplish these, there is need for one person to be in overall charge and to be ultimately accountable for decisions and outcomes. While essential, it is critical though to be aware of the weaknesses of the pyramid structure. These weaknesses are:

1. Over-dependence on a single leader

The leader is often assumed to be the most competent in terms of knowledge, skills and experience. As such, the team learns to over-rely on the leader to set the direction, plan the work, solve problems along the way and achieve the outcomes. In consequence, the leader often sits in the bus driver's seat to steer the team to meet expectations as the bottom-line is either to "perform or perish". In his absence, progress can falter, and the team become rudderless.

2. Passive team members

Continuing the bus analogy, team members learn to be supporting, but often become passive passengers while the leader is busy controlling the vehicle as it passes through the challenging terrain. They are conditioned to wait for the leader's instructions as it takes less effort to follow than to lead. Indeed, in some cases, they wanted to help drive the bus, but their leader did not allow them. Mary Parker Follett, a management consultant and social worker in the early 1900s who was dubbed the Prophet of Management by Peter Drucker, spoke about the inertia of team members who don't understand their role nor value their potential. "Most people are not for or against anything; the first object of getting people together is to make them respond somehow, to overcome inertia". Factors that contribute to this inertia include personality, workplace culture, upbringing, education and societal norms. This book is focused on how to enable teams to respond and to overcome their inertia.

The leader often sits in the bus driver's seat to steer the team to meet expectations as the bottom-line is to "perform or perish". In his absence, progress can falter, and the team become rudderless.

3. Rigid job descriptions

The leader establishes job descriptions so that team members know their roles, duties and responsibilities. Now it is critical that every employee, whatever his level, be clear about his role and how it is aligned with his superior and peers. However, the job description can have the unintended consequence of limiting the contributions and freedom of members, forming silos as a result. It boxes everyone within a mental boundary of what they can be and do. When it comes to job descriptions of the leader and members, it reinforces the notion that the role of team members is not to lead, but to simply support and assist the leader. Worse, the team members are not invited to participate in the formulation of their job descriptions. We can see the dangers in a typical job description which can limit people right from Day 1 when they started work with us.

- Team Manager:
  To ***lead***, direct, administer and control the day-to-day operations and activities of facilities and programs in your assigned functional area.

- Team Member:
  To ***support*** the Manager to achieve the work objectives, provide expertise in your area and complete your assigned tasks.

Pyramid under attack

The pyramid is under attack due to the below 4 challenges:

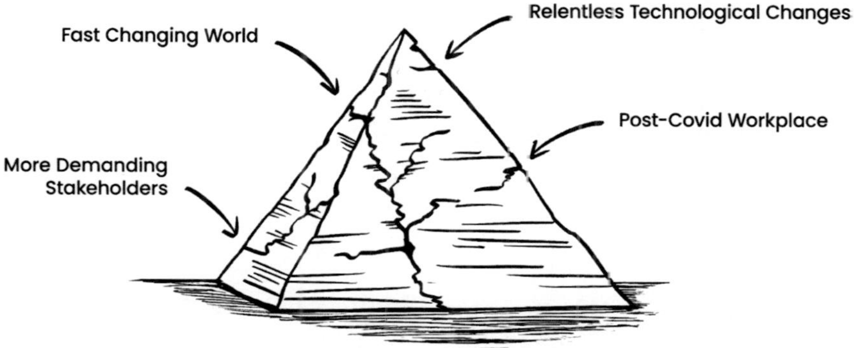

Figure 1-1: Traditional Pyramid Under Attack

1. Challenging leadership in a fast-changing world

Given the fast-changing world, which is becoming more and more volatile, uncertain, complex and ambiguous (VUCA), the notion that the leader alone is capable of leading the team has been challenged for some time now. No matter how transformational, visionary and capable our leaders are, they are after all humans. They are only able to do so much, even when performing at the highest level of leadership, be it in business, social enterprise, community or in government. They have practical limitations in terms of capability and capacity. The leadership shoe is becoming too big for any one person to wear alone.

The leadership shoe is becoming too big for any one person to wear alone.

In a study by Trollestad (2003) of 15 CEOs in Sweden, the CEOs agreed that a good leader is someone who is a mature, stable and balanced person. However, they acknowledged that this description is far from adequate. The reality is leaders are struggling with lack of time, stress and expectations from their stakeholders. Importantly, many fight to find the opportunity to achieve the necessary balance in the important areas in their lives. Their situation is shared by leaders across the world at all levels of the leadership hierarchy. Richard, a regional CEO of a global pharmaceutical company in Singapore, told us he worked 16 hours a day and often spends his weekend at work. We had a coaching session one Friday afternoon and he, working from home because of the Covid-19 pandemic, revealed that he had not left his apartment for the past 5 days -- since Monday that week. With 22 direct reports in Asia Pacific, he was certainly carrying a very heavy load on his shoulder. Many leaders face similar work pressure. Richard's response of working harder is not sustainable organizationally, professionally and personally, including his family and personal health.

2. More demanding stakeholders

Stakeholders, both inside and outside the organization, have become more demanding. Shareholders and bosses want to create higher value and have better results each year, often without providing the necessary resources required. One often-heard management catch-phrase is "do more, with less".

At the employees' end, team members are becoming harder to lead and less receptive to what they see as management 'dictates' into which they had little input. The Gen Y and its younger siblings, the Gen Z (collectively known as Millennials in this writing), look for meaningful purpose in their work. They seek workplaces whose purpose and mission resonate and align with them. They want to use their strengths and talents to contribute in a meaningful way. They also want the opportunity to be heard and to be paid attention to.

Joshua, the 20-year-old son of one of our Singaporean colleagues, applied for an internship as a software engineer. At the selection interview with the company, the hiring manager asked him what he looked for in his future employer. After a few moments of silence, he said there are three things that are important to him:

- His work must make a positive impact on society
- The company must have the right equipment for him
- He has the freedom to express himself

Some companies remain reluctant to accommodate the Joshuas of this world who want to have more say and control on what, and in how, they work. Other organizations, however, recognize that under wiser leadership, the team will thrive because of the passion and energy of the Joshuas. To ignore this passion, teams will miss out on the possibilities and creativity that the younger generations can generate.

3. The relentless technological transformation

The third pressure is caused by the relentless pace of technological transformation, commonly known as Industrial Revolution or IR 4.0. The turn of the 21st century has been remarkable. The world has witnessed breakthroughs in emerging technologies in fields such as robotics, artificial intelligence, nanotechnology, the internet of things, quantum computing, biotechnology, 3D printing, self-driving vehicles, 5Gs and now we are talking about 6Gs. Almost every sector is impacted by IR 4.0.

Many organizations have launched internal transformational strategies to remain competitive and relevant. They have seen how existing business models were disrupted by new entrants in the transportation, hotels, banking, retail, food & beverage sectors. Many of these new entrants were able to use digital technology to challenge the incumbent with great ferocity, even though they were newbies.

The pressure is not only coming from external competition. Internal challenges and their impact on employees must be addressed. While organizations want their workers to adapt quickly, they need to be sensitive to some workers being resistant to change, especially the older employees with their comfort zones. It is essential that the organization engages its workers and explain why and how the company support them as they confront change.

4. The post-Covid workplace

For more than 2 years, starting from the beginning of 2020, the world has been grappling with unprecedented change. Many countries were forced to repeatedly lock-down their cities in their quest to contain the virus spread.

The pandemic has changed the workplace in a permanent way. The extended period of working from home has shown many employees to be as productive at home as they were when operating in the office. At the same time, many employees have better balance in their work and personal lives. The several hours of commute that they saved each day have been allotted to "me-time" and personal interaction with their family. Many organizations have gravitated towards the hybrid mode where employees divide their time between working in the office and home. This adds to the challenge of team leadership.

In a research study published by the Harvard Business Review in July 2020, a survey of 1,200 people in 24 different countries showed that 40% of the 215 supervisors surveyed expressed low self-confidence in their ability to manage their team members remotely. They had negative views about their team members' performance. A similar proportion (38%) agreed that remote workers perform worse than if they had worked physically at the workplace. These results are not surprising. The traditional pyramid works well in-person, as everyone, including the leader, is physically accessible to each other, and in some cases, are just a shout away. When management by sight is removed, it becomes challenging to manage by trust.

The below Table 1-1 looks at the workplace before the Covid-19 pandemic and what a post-Covid workplace may look like.

	Pre-Covid-19 Workplace	The Post-Covid Workplace
1	Typically work 9 to 6 in the office.	Flexible time and place of work, so long as responsibilities and deliverables are fulfilled, and expectations met or exceeded.
2	Manage by sight. Important to be seen working. Focus on process and doing.	Manage by trust. Focus on results and outcomes and less on the process.
3	More homogeneous teams as members are hired from the local area.	More members are hired across borders as work can be done virtually, giving rise to more diversity in the team.
4	In-person meeting is the default mode. Virtual meeting is the exception.	Comfortable with virtual interactions. In-person meeting is only out of necessity or for specific purposes.
5	Clear professional career ladder and growth paths.	Employees have more career choices, creating their own portfolio of professional expertise, based on their passion and strengths.
6	Work is structured, pre-defined and organized.	Work is fluid, dynamic and employees step up where required.
7	Operate in unintended silos and lack of sharing information within and between teams, caused by over-focus on own functional or individual responsibilities.	Information is shared more freely as members readily speak up, allowing faster sharing and response to information within and between teams.
8	Team members take and act on orders and instructions.	Opportunity for any team member to initiate and participate in problem-solving and decision making.
9	Learning is about assimilating knowledge.	Learning is about assimilating and adapting existing knowledge and proactively creating new knowledge.
10	Focus on work needs & production. A work and result-oriented workplace.	Focus on the needs of the whole person as a human being. Both work and personal outcomes are emphasized, leading to a more humanized workplace and organization.

Table 1-1: Comparison between the Pre-Covid and Post-Covid Workplace

The Three Shifts

The foundations of the traditional pyramid have been shaky ever since we entered the 21st century. This was driven in part by the rise of automation and digitization, the democratization of information and a more demanding workforce. Nearly 20 years ago, Fletcher and Kaufer wrote about the 3 shifts in their book, "Shared leadership: Paradox and Possibility" (2003):

1. The Base is more important than the Top

- The notion of one single leader starts to diminish. An organization is like an iceberg, the base is more important than the top. Collective achievements and shared responsibility are more critical than the individual achievements of the leader and members.

2. Leadership is Social

- Leadership is a social activity and requires paying attention and engaging team members as social beings as members are also co-creators of leadership.

3. Leadership is Collective Learning

- Leadership is learning collectively for the leader and team to grow.

Leadership is a social activity and requires paying attention and engaging team members as social beings as members are also co-creators of leadership.

The bottom line: The pressures on team leaders caused by factors mentioned above, continue to increase year by year. The effects of the pandemic will reverberate globally for years, shaking the organizations further. The post-Covid-19 workplace will require leaders to view their leadership through a new mental model. Leadership styles will continue to flow towards more consultative, collaborative and people-centered approaches. There will also be increasing emphasis on coaching both teams and individuals, as they answer the organizations' needs for higher performance and the grooming of successors.

So What? …… Insights

Our view is that employee engagement still remains a substantial challenge. Numerous studies report that less than 20% of employees feel fully engaged in their work. This fact has serious implications for leadership attitudes and organizational productivity. It means that any leader desiring a higher performing team must develop the capability to engage and draw out the expertise and energy from the 80% of employees who are "not-fully engaged" or "disengaged" (the "quiet quitters"). A continuing leadership challenge will be to search for better and more effective ways to maximize the potential of every employee.

Any leader desiring a higher performing team must develop the capability to engage and draw out the expertise and energy from the 80% of employees who are "not-fully engaged" or "disengaged" (the "quiet quitters").

The CEO of one of the world's largest banks rightfully believed that if it was possible to increase employee engagement by just a few percentage points, they would outperform all the other banks. So, the Head of Learning and Development (L&D) of their Hong Kong bank invited us to speak to their top 80 leaders for four hours on this topic. We declined and said, "Does this sound like an engaging strategy? We can't speak for 4 hours on the topic; if we could, we wouldn't. However, we can co-design an engaging workshop with your L&D team so that at the end of a 4-hour workshop your top 80 managers will have written a booklet titled: ***"Increasing Employee Engagement in XYZ Bank: What we will do"***. And they did. All we need to do today is to create a safe, engaging environment for employees including leaders to speak up so the collective wisdom creates a solution from inside-out. The answers are inside everyone. We only need to help bring them to the surface.

In the next chapter, we will begin to look at the Shared Leadership way of leading. We believe this is what leaders and organizations need to bring out the best of their teams and employees to operate and win in this new and challenging world that we are in.

Shared Leadership - A Better Way To Lead & Coach

"The greatest danger in times of turbulence is not turbulence, it is to act with yesterday's logic"

Peter Drucker
Management Consultant & Educator

Shared leadership is very much like a team sport. We need the whole team to function together for success. To turn in high performance in each and every game, the team requires every member to take the lead at various times during the game. We don't expect the team captain to lead at every moment. All team members must take responsibility to share in the leading. As James Quigley, CEO Emeritus, Deloitte U.S. puts it: "The timeless challenge of leadership is to bring together a group of diverse individuals and create an environment where they will work together effectively toward common, shared goals."

What is shared leadership

The concept of shared leadership is not new. Many organizations practice it successfully. Leadership in Motion (LIM) has, since early 2000, coached leaders of its client organizations, in both the private and public arenas, to embrace the concept of sharing leadership. In essence, ***shared leadership is a leadership approach where leaders give more influence, power and ownership (IPO) to their team members, enabling them to speak up, step up and take on more leadership and ownership, with a higher sense of purpose.***

Figure 2-1: Geese flying

In essence, shared leadership is a leadership approach where leaders give more influence, power and ownership (IPO) to their team members, enabling them to speak up, step up and take on more leadership and ownership, with a higher sense of purpose.

Unlike conventional leadership models, which involve a leader exerting influence downwards, the concept of shared leadership entails the interchange of ideas and influence between peers working together in a team. Cox, Pearce & Perry in their 2003 paper "Toward a model of shared leadership and distributed influence in the innovation process" describe it as "a condition where teams collectively exert leadership influence". Critical to the effectiveness of shared leadership is the presence of shared purpose, mission and values among team members. This can be a challenge when a team comprises peers from different functions or teams, and thus commitment to the team's purpose and mission forms the glue that ensures the collective effectiveness. A clear added benefit of shared leadership is the resultant cohesion when all members learn and develop from the exposure to their colleagues' skills and knowledge, as they address their challenge.

Shared leadership is a powerful approach for the professional development of the future leaders and people in any organization. We have found that once leaders and HR professionals learn about shared leadership, they are confident at how it can positively impact their organization's culture, performance and succession plans.

Why sharing leadership is an effective way to lead & coach

Shared leadership is born out of necessity and from the wisdom of leaders that they themselves cannot possibly do everything on their own. Most experienced leaders in organizations such as multinational corporations, social, government, family businesses and start-ups, recognize that more heads are better than one. What is effective at the management level is also relevant to other levels of the organization. We believe it makes sense to cascade this way of leading and coaching from the senior leadership, down to the team level. We recommend this to our clients who understand the benefits of using this approach to bring out the best in their teams and to inculcate the next generation of leaders in the organization.

Shared leadership is an effective response to the 4 critical leadership challenges that we discussed in Chapter 1:

1. Challenging operating conditions and decisions in a faster-changing world
2. Increasing demands from stakeholders
3. The relentless technological transformation
4. The post-Covid workplace

As you can see from Table 2-1, shared leadership is advantageous to traditional pyramid leadership in 5 key aspects:

	Aspects	Traditional Leadership	Shared Leadership
1	Leadership of the team	Driven by the leader. Work and responsibilities are delegated downwards to members. Image: Team pyramid	Driven by both the leader and team members, based on the work and shared responsibilities. Members take initiatives to speak up and step up whenever needed. Image: Flying geese
2	Influence	The leader usually exerts influence from top-down to the team members.	Influence can be exerted from any team member to the leader or other team members, regardless of job role or level. Every voice is heard.
3	Power & Control	Power centrally held by the leader. The leader controls the steering wheel.	Team members are collectively empowered to take control of the steering wheel as the situation and work requires.
4	Mindset	The leader defines and owns the team goals and outcomes. Team members see themselves as "doers", responding to direction from the top.	Leader and team members share in the ownership of the team goals and outcomes, with members involved in the "thinking" as well as the "doing".
5	Motivation of members	The leader relies on extrinsic rewards as a transaction, in exchange for work to be produced. Depending on the leadership, members may also be motivated intrinsically.	Members are primarily motivated by the shared purpose, mission, autonomy, team environment, the growth opportunities and the quality of the leadership.

Table 2-1 Comparison of Traditional Leadership with Shared Leadership

From the above discussion, you have seen how shared leadership benefits the entire organization by addressing current challenges and opportunities—and by developing its people at the same time. Its central purpose is to harness and optimize the people power that you have. This is done not by directing them, but by creating the conditions that enable them to want to speak up, step up, take on greater leadership, increase ownership and by using all the tacit expertise and strengths that they collectively have.

Pre-requisites for implementing Shared Leadership

Typically, people climb the leadership ladder based on their technical expertise and their success in achieving their KPIs. Leaders who are strong in contributing to the bottom-line results are often seen as high performers. The recognition and rewards that they receive motivated them to drive the team even harder.

This almost singular focus on achieving organizational goals is fast changing. Organizations are increasingly recognizing and placing a higher premium on leaders who are able to inspire, galvanize and grow their people to achieve the organizational goals. In other words, leaders have to be bi-focused, concentrating on achieving organizational goals and creating the conditions for their people to be the best that they can be. An effective and sustainable answer is to share the leadership.

Leaders have to be bi-focused, concentrating on achieving organizational goals and creating the conditions for their people to be the best that they can be. An effective and sustainable answer is to share the leadership.

According to Cox, Pearce and Perry (2003) the ability to share leadership is based on the following 3 criteria:

1. Members understand their expectation to provide constructive influence to each other
2. Members accept responsibility to appropriately provide and respond to leadership from their peers
3. Members develop the skills to follow and to lead effectively

In other words, implementing shared leadership in your team will require the following:

1. The leader must first be "on-board"

For shared leadership to be successfully implemented, it is essential that the leader understands and is open to learning and experiencing the new approach. The leader holds the IPO (influence, power and ownership). Our experience has been that before they experience the benefits of shared leadership, some leaders are reluctant to embrace this leadership style. Understandably, some leaders feel that they have been given the role of team leader and that therefore the accountability for achieving team success rests with them. Not every leader accepts the notion of sharing their leadership. Others believe that their members will think less of them if they delegate too much influence and power downwards. You can read more in Chapter 14 where we discuss ways to help the leader to come on board.

2. Establish clear working norms and learn the tools

The second requirement is to define how the team wishes to work together and learning the shared leadership tools to make the approach work well. The requirement includes:

- Reaching agreement on the team's purpose, mission and outcomes
- Defining and accepting the behavioral norms by which the team members will work together

- Contracting between the team leader and team members about how they will work to achieve the team strategy and goals and specifying what each party requests of, and what each offers, to the other
- Learning and equipping the leader and the team members with the skills and tools to make the sharing of leadership easy, effective and enjoyable

3. Make shared leadership a new habit

The third requirement is for all members to be willing to step out of their comfort zone, to persevere in embracing the mindset, attitudes, behaviors and skills necessary to make the sharing of leadership come alive in the team. Every team will have settled into certain norms of behaviors. It will take time and effort to change. Just like a sapling that you plant in the soil, it will take time for the sapling to grow before it can flower and bear fruit. Similarly, the leader and team need to inculcate a learning discipline in the "doing" to see the noticeable changes in the team.

Creating the Right P.L.A.C.E.

The Covid-19 pandemic had caused many professionals and working people to hit the 'Pause" button and re-evaluate their job, career and life. One consequence of the pandemic is the "Great Resignation". First coined in 2021 in the US, it is a situation where employees are leaving their jobs in the millions in search for jobs that better fulfill or match their needs and wants.

Notwithstanding the "Great Resignation", organizations have always been dealing with employee resignations. One key reason for this turnover is people have not truly found the ***Right P.L.A.C.E.*** There are 5 essential elements of a right P.L.A.C.E.:

- **Purpose** — A right place is where there is clear purpose or reason "why" I am working in this team or organization. The "why", when it is clearly aligned with the employees, make the job meaningful and purposeful.

- **Leadership** — A right place is one where enlightened leaders create the space for excellence, sharing their influence, power & ownership with the team. Leaders who share their leadership will create the environment for the right place to be realized.

- **Autonomy** — A right place is where employees have the ability to control and manage their work, and their lives. With clear expectations on the "what" that needs to be done, the "how" and "where" work is done can be decided by the team members. The hybrid work arrangement, where employees apportion their time to work in the office or at home, is motivating to people because they have better control over their work and life.

- **Connections** — A right place is one where there is a warm and caring team environment. Everyone feels connected with and among each other, knowing each other as human beings and not "human doings". Being connected brings up the human spirit in each person and in the team.

- **Endowments** — A right place is one that allows the employees to make the most use of their endowments. These include their strengths, talents and competencies. It is the place that allows members to play to their strengths and shine. The opportunities and space to learn, grow and expand their strengths and talents are also part of the social contract in the right place.

These are 5 key factors that inspire people to excellence, from the inside out. People who found the Right P.L.A.C.E. has less reason to move elsewhere. The good news is every leader is able to create the Right P.L.A.C.E. for their people using the Shared Leadership Disciplines® described in this book.

So What? …… Insights

Whenever we talk about sharing leadership to leaders and team coaches, there are often nods of agreement and "Yes, why not!". Almost everyone can see and feel the logic and common sense. There will also be some leaders and coaches who will have less confidence in its workability, and require more time to accept the change. This is part of the learning and change process.

Shared leadership will work when leaders are willing to be open to learning and embracing a better way to lead and to coach the team. It is acknowledging that the ability to bring out the best of the team and the individual members will be a key leadership differentiator in today's fast changing world. With our more than 30 years working with organizations and teams in this field, our experience is that shared leadership can work in the different societal cultures. We have seen it operate successfully in various countries, spanning the Americas, Africa, Europe and Asia. In other words, shared leadership is a way of leading that transcends geographies and cultures. Its attractiveness lies in its intrinsic motivation that every human being yearns for, chief among which, is the autonomy and space, the opportunity to learn and grow, and having meaning and purpose in the work.

The ability to bring out the best of the team and the individual members will be a key leadership differentiator in today's fast changing world.

By now you have a clear understanding of the “what” and “why” of shared leadership. Before we show you the “how” in Part 2, Chapter 3 will help you understand how shared leadership has evolved over the past 100 years.

CHAPTER 3

The Evolution of Shared Leadership

> **"Leadership is not defined by the exercise of power but by the capacity to increase the sense of power among those led. The most essential work of the leader is to create more leaders."**

Mary Parker Follett
Management Consultant, Social Worker

The study of leaders and leadership has intrigued mankind for hundreds and thousands of years in many parts of the world. Going back to ancient history, we have learned about leadership from philosophers and thinkers such as Confucius, Lao Tzu, Sun Tzu, Socrates, Plato, Machiavelli, Peter Drucker and many others.

Leadership concepts and practices

The most essential work of the leader is to create more leaders.

Interestingly, the term "leadership" has only been in existence since the late 1700s (Stogdill,

1974). Since then, various leadership concepts and practices evolved into the present age. This evolution of leadership thoughts can be summarized into 6 eras (Albert, 1990):

1. Personality Traits Era (1860s-1940s)

The first social scientific study of leaders was by Francis Gallon, a scientist and researcher, who wrote a book ***Hereditary Genius*** in 1869. His idea was that leaders are born and not made. The influence was nature and not nurture. For many years, the focus was on hereditary and personality traits, emphasizing the great leadership heroes. The universality of the traits approach was challenged in the mid-20th century as there were difficulties getting wide agreement on a set of consistent leadership traits and attributes across a variety of situations.

2. Behavioral Era (1950s-1970s)

Instead of focusing on traits and power, the Behavioral Era focused on what leaders do. It was concluded that understanding how leaders behave will enable these behaviors to be copied by other leaders. Studies were on the impact of leaders' concern for tasks and people. The study of how leaders use reinforcement to shape desired subordinate behaviors was also the highlight of this era. The Michigan Leadership Studies, Ohio State Leadership Studies and Blake & Mouton Managerial Grid Model were developed during this period.

3. Situation or Contingency Era (1950s-1980s)

The Situation Era acknowledges that leadership is not one-dimensional. Other factors were involved, beside the dynamics between the leader and the subordinates. The premise was that leadership is contingent on factors of behavior, personality, influence and situation in order for managers to create effective leadership and impact. Hersey-Blanchard Situational Leadership and Path-Goal Theory are good examples.

4. Transactional Era (1970s-1980s)

The Transactional Era studies leadership as a system of exchange of rewards and penalties. It focuses on role differentiation and social interaction between the leader and the members. The Dyad Linkage Theory (Dansereau, Graen, and Haga, 1975) was a good example that was developed in this era.

5. Transformational & Culture Era (1980s - the present)

The focus of the Transformational & Culture Era is based on the environment and on leaders providing intrinsic, rather than extrinsic, motivation. The central idea is leaders should exercise their influence to produce enthusiastic commitment by their members as opposed to using compliance. When leaders can create a strong culture within the team or organization, employees will be able to lead themselves. The role of leaders is to inspire and motivate their members for higher performance.

Leadership is evolving and will continue to evolve in the future as we face our changing operating environment, new technological development, changing expectations of society and improvement in our knowledge and understanding of human needs and motivation. The evolution will be towards finding innovative solutions to address society's current and future opportunities and challenges.

The historical bases of Shared Leadership

As leadership concepts were evolving as described above, the desires to gain higher motivation and performance through the increased involvement and participation from their members were also emerging. These form the genesis of the shared leadership style. The key historical bases for shared leadership include:

1. "Law of the Situation" (1920s)

Mary Parker Follett was credited by many to be the mother of shared leadership. She introduced the idea of the "Law of the Situation" in 1925 where people should follow the person with the most knowledge of the situation at hand and not just the person with the formal authority. To her, leadership is power with others, rather than power over others. In her words, "part of the task of the leader is to make others participate in his leadership. The best leader knows how to make his followers actually feel power themselves, not merely acknowledging his power".

2. Participation in decision making (1960s)

Employee participation in decision-making has long been an interest to scholars and researchers since the late 1960s. Much research has been conducted on the effects of employee participation to productivity and satisfaction. The participation focuses on the work, typically dealing with how it is organized, what is done and who does what.

The best leader knows how to make his followers actually feel power themselves, not merely acknowledging his power.

In a study entitled "Employee Participation: Diverse Forms and Different Outcomes", Dachler and Wilpert (1978) analysis of previous research studies showed the following results:

- Employee participation that has high access, and is direct and long term, leads to higher performance and productivity.
- Direct forms of participation, for example with employees directly involved in work decisions, or having the ability to influence decision-making (e.g. on work matters) have shown

greater effectiveness than indirect forms where the employee views are represented by others.

- Informal employee participation leads to overall job satisfaction. Every study that examined satisfaction with supervisors (10 out of 10 studies) and/or satisfaction with work itself (5 out of 5 studies), positive associations were found with informal participation (defined as non-statutory consensus emerging among interacting members).

3. Vertical Dyad Linkage (1970s)

Another early shared leadership concept was the Vertical Dyad Linkage or the Leader-Member Exchange Theory that was developed by George Graen in the 1970s. For the leader to increase the personal commitment and sense of ownership of the team members, the leader should "offer the member wider latitude in his role, more leadership attention, greater support and larger influence on the unit's operation" (Dansereau et. al. 1975).

There are 3 stages in the Vertical Dyad Linkage process:

1. Role taking
2. Role making
3. Role stabilization

In the role taking stage, the leader communicates to the members, making clear their responsibilities and what is expected of them. The members carry out their work and find opportunities to show their capabilities and contributions and, in the process, allow the leader to observe their capabilities.

Employee participation that has high access, and is direct and long term, leads to higher performance and productivity.

This is followed by the role making stage where, based on the manner in which members take on and perform their roles, the members will be managed and treated differently by the leader. The outcome is not the same for all the team members as it depends on the individual responses of each member at the role taking stage and the subjective perception and assessment by the leader. Over time, based on the members' responses, they are eventually and arbitrarily categorized as the "in-group" and an "out-group" by the leader, depending on his experiences and assessment. The "in-group" were those who stepped up when given the opportunity by the leader. As such, they were trusted more by the leader and given more responsibilities and opportunities as compared to the "out-group".

In the role stabilization stage, the in-group and out-group settle down in their role relationships, norms and routines on how work is consulted, collaborated and done.

4. Self-leadership & Empowerment (1980s - 1990s)

Leaders can emerge from a leaderless group, even when not appointed or elected as a leader (Bartol and Martin, 1986). When the situation dictates, any member can step up as the leader within the group to take on a certain task or even the team leadership role. The leader emerges from the consensus and support of the rest of the team members, and is not decreed by the bosses. Teams that decide their own leaders demonstrate higher commitment to success to ensure their leader succeed as their leader.

A more organized version is the self-managed work teams which have grown in popularity since their introduction in the 1960s. A self-managed team is a group of employees which is responsible and accountable for solving problems, increasing quality, productivity, innovation and creative solutions. Its popularity grows in line with the exponential growth of the internet. With employees who are better informed, self-motivated, self-directed and are specialists, and know more than their managers, teams have less need for their manager's supervision and direction.

5. Shared Leadership (2000s)

Shared leadership recognizes that leadership can come from any member of the team, and not necessary from the positional authority of the leader. The term "Shared Leadership" started to be used more widely from the 2000s. Leadership In Motion (LIM) LLC co-pioneered a reflective and integrative form of action learning with the Swedish MiL Institute in the early 1980s. This became known as Action Reflection Learning® as LIM built on it with more development, experimentation and adaption of various tools and processes while working with, and coaching leaders in various parts of the world. LIM's work with leaders then, and now, is to enable them to share more of their influence, power and ownership (IPO) with their teams. This means hearing every member's voice and providing a safe space and conducive environment for their members to step up and take on more leadership to achieve the team's performance and outcomes. Since early 2000, our coaches have been advocating leaders to intentionally build "shared leadership teams", tapping into the intrinsic motivation, capabilities and tacit knowledge of every member in their team, rather than keeping them "subordinated" and be mere "followers".

Shared leadership recognizes that leadership can come from any member of the team, and not necessary from the positional authority of the leader.

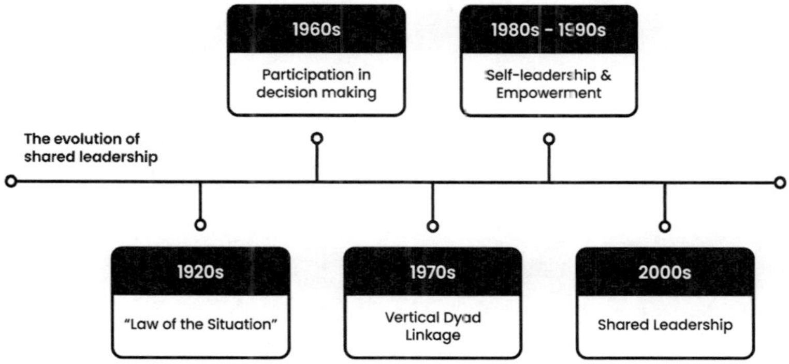

Figure 3-1: Time line of shared leadership evolution.

About the same time, two related concepts were also developed: distributed leadership and collective leadership.

Distributed Leadership

The aim of distributed leadership is to decentralize leadership as much as possible without the leader suffering any loss of formal positional authority. One key motivation of distributed leadership is to lessen the load of leaders. It gained a lot of attention in the 2000s, particularly in the US education sector. With increased workload faced by principals, leadership responsibilities were distributed to the teachers, and this helped relieve the pressure on the principals (Lashway, 2003). The leader's role in distributed leadership is to create shared common cause, common values and common goals and at the same time, actively delegate and assign responsibilities to the members.

Collective Leadership

Collective leadership is based on the notion of "joint" leadership where participants jointly work together to achieve the collective goals. It is a community where members lead themselves. Healthcare is one sector that is at the forefront of collective leadership. The interdependence in healthcare necessitates a more collective leadership approach to improving the quality of decisions and patient safety. This is opposed to the hierarchical approach of a formal leader bearing the responsibilities for decision-making. Collective leadership enables leaders to work together more seamlessly, be it in or outside their professional, functional, team, organizational or even geographical boundaries. It allows multi-disciplinary teams to function well, bringing in diverse views, different expertise and values to tackle the complex and challenging issues in medical diagnosis and treatment.

West et al. in the Journal of Organizational Effectiveness (2014) said it well: "In collective leadership cultures, responsibility and accountability function simultaneously at both individual and collective levels. They breed regular reflective practice focused on failure, organizational learning and making continuous improvement an organizational habit. By contrast command and control leadership cultures invite the displacement of responsibility and accountability onto a single individual, leading to scapegoating and a climate of fear of failure rather than an appetite for innovation".

Shared leadership is gaining a lot of ground in organizations all over the world. As testified by the large number of leaders and teams whom we have coached, the results of shared leadership spoke for themselves. We believe more and more leaders will embrace shared leadership as the better way to lead and coach.

So What? …… Insights

This brief overview shows how different leadership thoughts and approaches have evolved over the last 100 years, and how the notion of shared leadership emerged almost a century ago, starting with Mary Follett. Even as far back as the 1960s, research reports on Participative Decision Making showed that team members who had more involvement, control and ownership of their work challenges performed better, and had better job engagement and satisfaction. What this means is the needs and wants of people to have a work environment that allows them to speak up and step up have existed for years. The voices are louder with the Gen Y and Gen Z. Senior management and team leaders are finding that with the right leadership mindset, framework and skills, they will be able to create a culture and environment that allows each and every team member to be

Team members who had more involvement, control and ownership of their work challenges performed better, and had better job engagement and satisfaction.

purposefully engaged, giving their best contributions and adding leadership bench strength to their organization.

In Part 1, Chapters 1 and 2 have provided you the "What" and "Why" Shared Leadership is a better way to lead and coach. Chapter 3 gives you the historical perspective, that for the last 100 years, leaders and researchers have always been figuring out how to enable employees to not only be active team players, but also as proactive partners, giving their full engagement and commitment to the team.

To us, we have a gem that has been partially hidden in the closet, and not many leaders and organizations have experienced its tremendous benefits. This gem is our 5 Shared Leadership Disciplines® built on the foundation of 10 Action Reflection Learning (ARL®) principles and supported by a wide range of ARL® tools and processes to bring the sharing of leadership to life. The pandemic has caused a sea change in the way we lead and the way that our people want to be led. People want to have more control and to be managed less. They want to be given more influence, power and a greater sense of purpose and ownership. We feel the time is ripe for the gem to be brought into the open through this book, and letting it be the guiding light for sustained team and organizational effectiveness and outcomes.

In Part 2, we will examine "how" you can implement shared leadership using the 5 Shared Leadership Disciplines®.

Part 2

The 5 Shared Leadership Disciplines

The Discipline of Connect

"Invisible threads are the strongest ties"

Friedrich Nietzsche
German Philosopher & Author

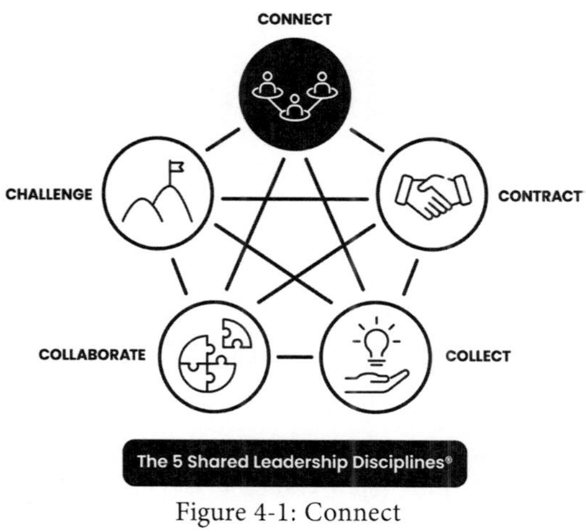

Figure 4-1: Connect

As the quote suggest we are not alone on this planet, in our communities, or as members of a team. By deeply connecting we can be more effective and more productive than if we worked alone.

What does the Discipline of *Connect* mean?

Connect is more than simply making contact. It requires getting to know team members at more than a superficial level. The purpose is to ensure that team members establish positive, appreciative and respectful relationships with one another at both the personal and professional levels. By so doing, we can foster a working environment that is safe, inspiring and fun. Research has found that teams who constantly invest time connecting - getting to know one another at different dimensions - are better able not only to survive but to thrive in tough times. We've all heard the saying, "when the going gets tough, the tough get going". Well, 'toughening' teams is part of the shared leadership work. Teams need to create opportunities to get to know one another - interests, likes, dislikes, family, values, feelings, dreams - actually, anything that is important, engaging and meaningful to the members. The curiosity, openness, warmth and caring for each other's personal lives will lead to interpersonal relationships, deeper trust and sometimes to deep friendships.

The curiosity, openness, warmth and caring for each other's personal lives will lead to interpersonal relationships, deeper trust and sometimes to deep friendships.

Besides connecting personally, it is also important for each team member to demonstrate connection and agreement with the team's purpose, mission, values, strategy, plans, norms and key processes. Team members need to understand how they are connected to the organization, the business and the planet. It is only when the leader enables his team members to connect in their head, heart and gut will they be able and willing to give their best. Anything less weakens the leader's ability to share leadership. ***Connect*** is the first step to engagement and why we have established it as the first **C.**

Why is connecting a discipline?

LIM's experience over the years has been that solid connections between co-workers, even those of long-standing, tend to be focused narrowly on the exchange of work-related information, and concentrated on each worker's functional interests. While this may be a natural pattern, we believe that failure to broaden connections, within and outside teams, can lead to lowered productivity and a lessened understanding of the organization's wider strategic needs. The advantages of gaining fuller knowledge of other teams, functions and stakeholders are both obvious and easily achieved if team members actively seek opportunities to connect with them. Currently when large numbers of employees are working outside the office, it is increasingly important for teams to take deliberate steps to maximize meaningful connections between all levels and all functions of the organization. We have developed with our clients simple but impactful ways to do this.

How can we promote connecting?

Connecting frequently happens accidentally. Every day we have accidental - usually casual and unplanned - opportunities to connect with members of our team or organization. Accidental face-to-face encounters frequently take place during breaks, over lunch, in the coffee room, in the hallways, during carpooling, etc. Virtual accidental encounters can take place via social media – responding to someone's post on Twitter, Instagram, Facebook, LinkedIn, Viber, WeChat, WhatsApp, Skype, Clubhouse, Telegram, Signal, emails, getting a phone call on one topic and using that as an opportunity to

At the beginning of every meeting in our team, we make it a habit to reserve 10 minutes or so for a personal check-in.

segue into another topic by offering an observation or sharing a story with a 'by the way, do you have another couple of minutes? Or 'let's meet tomorrow for a virtual coffee' and then proceed into a deeper 'connecting' conversation. Once we realize how valuable and beneficial connecting is in building relationships, we can be more intentional to make the most of these accidental opportunities.

Connecting can also be the result of design. Here are four ways we recommend you try out:

1. Check-In

One of the easiest and most effective ways to connect intentionally is to establish a meeting 'check-in' ritual. At the beginning of every meeting in our team, we make it a habit to reserve 10 minutes or so for a personal check-in. One person on the team is asked to prepare a 'check in' question, most often of a personal nature, and separate from items on the agenda. These questions need to be open ended and catalysts for quick stories. Everyone is given a minute or so to find a story related to the check-in question; then we take turns sharing our stories. Depending upon the time available and the number of the people in the meeting we allocate from 30 seconds to 3 minutes per person for connecting. Invariably, these stories become memorable moments, build appreciation, open opportunities for deeper conversations and build empathy that can lead to laughter or tears and topics for future conversations. Each check-in is an opportunity for discovery of our colleagues, and even of ourselves.

Here are a few of the 'check in' questions we have used:

- "What's 'new or news' outside of my work?"
- "What is something I am grateful for recently?"
- "How am I feeling right now and why?"
- "What do I do to keep myself physically fit?"
- "What is one new learning for me recently?"
- "What's my next holiday plan?"

There are literally hundreds of great check-in questions. We have provided 30 great check-in questions at the back of this book.

Rotate this 'check-in' role among all team members along with other meeting roles like timekeeper, notetaker, coach, meeting organizer and meeting facilitator. A good check-in can achieve the following:

a. Establish a relaxed tone for the meeting.
b. Hear everyone's voice at the very beginning of a meeting.
c. Appreciate different aspects of your team members.
d. Discover something that you would never have expected about a team member.
e. Open topics to tag for more in-depth conversations later.

2. Extended Coffee Breaks

We were invited by one of Singapore's business schools several years ago to give a 4-hour talk on leadership to the board members of a Nigerian IT start-up who happened to be meeting for the first time with their sister company in Singapore. We convinced the business school that a workshop on leadership would be better than a lecture. The team comprised 12 men, 10 Nigerians and 2 Swiss lawyers. The room we were given was the boardroom in one of Singapore's 5-star hotels. This was not ideal as we prefer to work in settings where it is easier to hold informal conversations. (Boardrooms are so named, someone observed, because they can be very boring places!) Indeed, the group was expecting a lecture. When we told them that we wanted to make our 4 hours engaging they looked at one another radiating resistance and surprise. They had not been advised that their 'lecture' had been turned into a 'workshop'. We asked them to introduce themselves by telling one thing that was unique to them and a question they wanted to explore in our workshop. We gave them a few minutes to prepare their introductions.

Their introductions brought the meeting to life, and they seemed to genuinely learn new insights about one another. They seemed to like their questions and appeared ready for the workshop we had designed: an extended coffee break followed by a series of mini dialogues around their questions; an informal 'work' session in small groups addressing some of their more 'actionable' questions; and ending with a summary, next steps and debrief.

After about an hour of introductions around the board room table we felt the group was ready for a deeper conversation. It was time to get out of the board room, so we suggested a coffee break of 30 minutes. The group looked at us as though we weren't sure what we were doing. We reassured them that this was what we intended as we stood up and invited them to join us in the large hallway for a coffee break.

Just as we anticipated – they broke into twos and threes and quickly moved into deep conversations while enjoying the pastries, fruit and coffee.

After 30 minutes of lively conversation, we invited them to join us in a circle near the coffee area to share some of the highlights of their informal exchange. As we went around the circle there was great interest in sharing insights. One group of three individuals raised a new question that hadn't come up in the boardroom – "How will we resist the temptation to become corrupted like so many other board members in other companies in Nigeria?" We stayed in the circle for another 30 minutes as this question was discussed with all members participating. When we returned to the boardroom table the ambience and level of intimacy had significantly shifted. It was a different group. They were more open, honest and eager to explore some of the other questions that had been raised earlier.

Lesson learned – create natural ways for a group to connect and learn from one another. Never underestimate the power of social learning over a break of some kind. The essence of 'happy hour' is not the beverage (although this certainly helps). It's the conversation. Our role is to create opportunities and stimulating environments for people to speak up.

3. Walk & Talk

A few years ago, one of our clients invited us to design and facilitate an offsite workshop for their small team of six. We learned that two of the team members had not been speaking to one another for more than a year. In every team meeting they sat as far apart from one another as possible and did not look at one another. The team was barely functioning because of the caustic relationship between the two.

On day one we designed a ***Walk & Talk*** exercise after lunch. *Walk & Talk* is exactly what the name connotes - an opportunity to walk and talk in pairs to increase the connection with, and appreciation of each teammate. Very often as team members we really don't connect at a personal level while we are in team meetings or even between meetings. We planned our exercise to involve all in the large group, but with members separating every 10 minutes into pairs, and walking with enough distance between pairs for a private conversation. Our off-site location was in a beautiful setting along the coast. The entire exercise was timed to take 90 minutes including a debrief at the end. There were two of us coaches and 6 team members. That made 7 rounds of 10 minutes per round. Every 10 minutes one of the coaches blew a whistle, and everyone rotated partners. At the end of 70 minutes, we all had a personal conversation with everyone in the group, talking about whatever we wanted.

At the end of our walk, we stood in a circle and debriefed our experience, exchanging insights and how we might apply the process later. Of course, we were all curious about the two men in the team who had not been speaking with one another.

To our pleasant surprise they opened the debrief. One of them admitted being very anxious since they would have to confront one another. However, they felt happy and relieved that they both agreed to see how this exercise might address their blocked relationship. One of them began their conversation by saying, "Do you remember why we've not been talking to one another for all this time?" The other gentleman said, "No, I can't remember, but it's time we got our act together and started behaving like adults. Ten minutes was not enough time, so we've agreed to have breakfast together tomorrow morning and continue our conversation." The rest of the team gave them a standing ovation.

We have witnessed repeatedly the power of this simple tool to open team members up for meaningful conversations. The coaches also benefitted from this 1:1 time with each team member to connect as well as to offer feedback, ask for feedback, explore emerging questions, provide coaching insights, and learn more about each member of the team. It is a priceless activity to help everyone connect with everyone on the team. It is usually rated as the most valuable event in a workshop or meeting. We created a similar concept based on this tool called "Coffee Connect". Every so many minutes with a musical signal from us like in Musical Chairs, individuals would meet another person in the room and stand or sit for a time to connect until the music started again.

4. Stories

We all grew up with stories. Our mothers, fathers, uncles, aunts, grandmothers, grandfathers, friends, religious leaders and teachers told stories. We heard stories on TV, radio and in our places of worship. We read stories in books, newspapers and journals. The Qur'an, the Bible, the Vedas, the Tanakh, the Upanishads, the Hadiths, the Agamas and the Tripitakas also offer stories for learning and living. Even social media offers us great stories. And for good reasons. Stories are easy ways to convey meaning, to facilitate learning and make learning memorable and fun. In our work as leaders and coaches we can do the same in our interventions.

One of the simple ways that we do this is to schedule adequate time at the beginning of any team intervention to allow the individuals to tell their personal stories to the other members on their team. Why do we do this? Most team members know very little about their other team members' personal lives. It gives everyone a chance to speak and be heard. One team member said that connecting with and learning more about his teammates was the highlight of his first team encounter. We have three variations that allow people to connect in different situations:

a. One Slide

One Slide allows every individual to tell his or her story illustrated by one slide only using pictures, drawings or figures - NO words are permitted. Most of us are better at remembering pictures; we don't have photographic memories for words. We can provide the words to the pictures to tell our story.

Most team members know very little about their other team members' personal lives. It gives everyone a chance to speak and be heard.

We recently started one of our TCCPs (Team Coach Certification Program®) by asking every person – participants and staff – to send in advance one slide with three pictures responding to the following three questions:

i.. What is something that you are proud of?

ii. What is something that is unique to you - a characteristic or experience that makes you unique in our group?

iii. What is one adjective that best describes you and why?

Everyone then had 2 minutes in our first session to tell three short stories using their picture slide. There were 25 of us and we finished in 50 minutes, giving 10 minutes for a short debrief. Without exception this exercise has proven invaluable as a critical team development step to help everyone connect.

b. OurStory

OurStory is a 'substitute' for History (His Story) which all too often is the way history has been formally recorded. Two of our coaches were recently working virtually with a team. The team leader was very vocal and indicated that he would present his version of the team's history and the significant events that over time shaped the team and its culture. He wanted to begin the workshop by recounting his version of what happened the year before. The coaches persuaded him to create ***OurStory*** by inviting every member of the team to add their significant events and insights from the time they joined the team. The results were amazing.

Everyone on that team of 10 was given time to think and identify two significant events that over the last year had a major impact on the team. One of the coaches introduced how to use the Zoom's whiteboard. She also drew a horizontal line across the middle of the whiteboard and 4 vertical lines representing the year's 4 quarters. Everyone was given a different pen color and 3 minutes to write the title of their two significant events and place them above the line in the quarter they occurred. Then below the line they wrote one word to describe the insight from that event. The facilitating coach then called upon everyone, one at a time, following the timeline to briefly tell their short story and insights within 4 minutes. After listening to all the stories and insights, they moved into a dialogue to extract deeper meaning. Then they took 10 minutes using Chat to identify what they would a) continue, b) start or do more and c) stop or do less. As the session was recorded, they had an audio file and a screenshot of ***OurStory*** as a document of their collective efforts. Two team members agreed to edit and organize the 'continue, start, stop' comments for a decision session at their next meeting.

The team leader was amazed and encouraged with the results. Yes, he had an opportunity to share what he considered to be key events. However, he, like everyone else, realized that they would not have uncovered what was 'significant' to every team member

IF they were not invited to speak up. In fact, during the dialogue several mentioned how this was an easy, non-threatening, effective and efficient way to give and receive feedback. By the way, this story-telling exercise had a significant impact on creating a learning culture – ensuring that every voice matters. When we work with a team face-to-face, we use flip charts and colored markers in the very same way. At the end of this exercise everyone is more connected with the team and its history. Even new members feel they are part of the team's history.

c. Memorable Moments or 'Catch of the Day'

Mealtime can be a rich opportunity to connect with our families while enjoying a meal together. However, all too often we hear that mealtime is an occasion to connect – not with family, but with friends using smart phones and social media. If this is the case in your family, here's how you can turn dinner time into a memorable part of the day and a time to connect with every member of your family.

It's really very easy. With our families we routinely try out one of two activities over dinner:

Memorable Moments – We take a minute or two to reflect over the day and identify two or three memorable moments and take turns sharing them stating why. Very often different family members have shared the same moment but have a different reason which enriches that experience for the others. This can apply equally to kids who have been in school and grandparents who have been around the house all day. We all have moments during the day that stand out for one reason or another. By asking an engaging question we get engaging answers. All too often we ask 'dead end' questions. Here are a few with the answers: "How was school today?" 'Just fine, please pass the potatoes.' Or "Did you have a good day at the office?" 'Yes, how was your day, honey?' Instead, consider having each person share ONE memorable moment and rotate the responses so that everyone is ensured a time to respond.

Catch of the Day – This is an opportunity for everyone to share their catch of the day (questions and insights of the day) that can bring any dinner to life. Several years ago, one of our coaches was celebrating New Year in Argentina with his wife and her family. His mother, Marge, was suffering from terminal cancer yet decided to join them if she could be excused from all late meals. Most meals in Argentina begin around 10 pm. She was accustomed to taking her meals around 5 pm and then off to bed. The extended family all agreed to meet around 8 pm for a pre-dinner drink and exchange of the 'Catch of the Day' – the questions that each person planned to bring to dinner as catalysts for some good stories – so Marge could at least hear what would serve as dinner entertainment later in the evening. All showed up for drinks including Marge. All shared their question with the others. They were so interesting that Marge decided to join them at 10pm for dinner. During a 2-hour meal in the hotel restaurant that was filled with guests, everyone at the coach's table was engaged in exchanging questions and stories. With 5 questions they told 25 stories over their New Year meal. Pain and sleep had disappeared. No one could have even imagined that Marge was celebrating her last New Year's dinner.

We have used both activities with teams to extend the team bonding and connecting opportunities.

Now you have learned a few ways to increase personal connections at work as well as at home. There are many more. We invite you to try some of these out and see what happens.

So What? …… Insights

Here are the key 'connecting' insights:

Effective Connecting……

- Begins and continues the never-ending trust-building process
- Creates bonds that helps teams stick together during tough times
- Strengthens links with colleagues and families which is essential when working virtually
- Deepens cross-functional awareness of challenges facing colleagues
- Brings joy to the job. We are with our colleagues, as much as, if not more than our families. We should seek to enjoy our work and our colleagues. Connecting helps
- Is engaging and can happen virtually as well as face-to-face
- Can happen accidentally or 'by design'
- Is the foundation of our 5 Shared Leadership Disciplines®

Now let's move to the Discipline of Contract.

The Discipline of Contract

"Don't make assumptions. Find the courage to ask questions and to express what you really want. Communicate with others as clearly as you can to avoid misunderstandings, sadness, and drama."

Don Miguel Ruiz
Mexican author

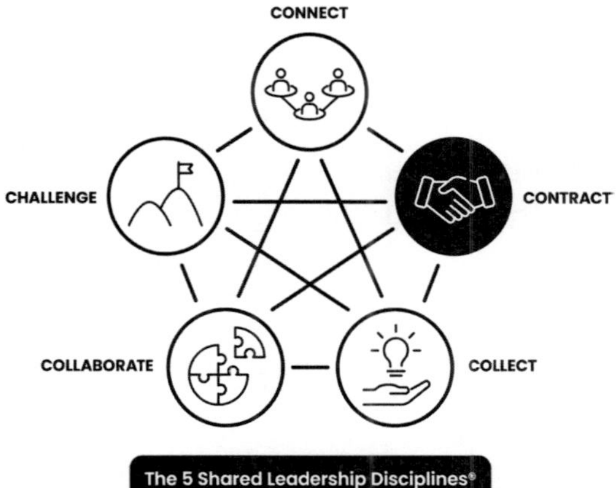

Figure 5-1: Contract

This quote gets at the heart of this chapter: Ask for what you want. All too often we get stuck in our own assumptions or what we believe others expect of us and all we need to do is ask, "What do you want?" or say, "Here's what I would like."

As in the previous chapter we begin with our definition of ***Contracting***. We follow with our rationale on why contracting is important and why it is often neglected. Then we briefly describe how contracting can happen on six different dimensions, with a focus on the team dimension. We then provide three short stories to illustrate some of the tools we use in the contracting process. We end with some suggested next steps and insights.

What does the Discipline of *Contract* involve?

The discipline of ***Contract*** is getting alignment, agreement and commitment around expectations of work and relationships. For optimal results this needs to happen on 6 dimensions: Personal; Professional; Team; Organizational; Business & Sustainability (environmental / societal). High performing teams clarify expectations in each of these dimensions. These expectations, when properly contracted become explicit, written commitments that lead to higher trust, better performance, greater profitability, less stress and more fun. Contracting is an on-going practice that involves defining, aligning, designing, assigning, refining, performing and supporting. To Contract is to commit and gain accountability.

The discipline of Contract is getting alignment, agreement and commitment around expectations of work and relationships.

At the **Personal Dimension**, contracting pertains to the team member's personal needs - family time, exercise, reading, journaling, writing, rest, recreation and other interests. It is about ensuring the team member has the space to meet their personal needs and obligations and it is key for the boss and the team members to agree mutually on their norms and expectations. This is especially crucial when working remotely as the boundary between work and personal time is often blurred.

At the **Professional Dimension**, it is essential that each team member, and his team leader or supervisor, clarify their mutual expectations regarding performance expectations, desired behavior, feedback, learning and career growth. Many companies' performance review processes are inadequate and often leave underperforming employees feeling disappointed, sad, angry and unfairly treated. We believe that performance evaluations should be an on-going process, and not a dreaded event every twelve months. They should include full participation by the employee; agreement on how performance will be judged; and regular opportunities throughout the year for shorter reviews to gauge if the goals and measurements are still relevant. All too often, performance conversations lead to even lower performance, dismissal, sabotage or departure. Most of these negative outcomes can be remedied by 'simply' establishing clarity on performance expectations and the supports required of the supervisor.

At the **Organizational Dimension**, each leadership team needs to define and get alignment within the organization and functional teams on culture, values, structure, policies, resources and key processes. Leadership teams must, in turn, get overall alignment on the same categories at cross-functional and cross-business levels as well as any other team that could be considered a 'key stakeholder'. For example, marketing and sales teams frequently have overlapping areas that could cause duplication or even 'no action' from either party. They might also need to solicit the expectations of the local, regional or global leadership teams depending on the situation. Every team must be aware of their key stakeholders inside the organization whose interests, opinions and requests need to be considered.

At the **Business Dimension**, each team must be vigilant to constantly ensure that it is aligned with, and committed to, the organization's (owner's) vision and strategy. This will ensure that the team performance and goals will contribute effectively to the organization's targets. As in the organization dimension, customers and suppliers as well as government entities may need to be considered and engaged.

At the **Sustainability Dimension** there are three critical questions to keep in mind:

1. What will we do to ensure that our business practices move from compliance to creative collaboration to protect and enhance our planet?
2. What will we do to support, challenge and protect our employees, customers, suppliers, vendors and those communities where we have plants, offices and people?
3. How will we maintain the momentum that we have created so that we are self-sufficient and constantly growing and learning across the other five dimensions?

The above 6 dimensions form the Pentagon-Plus System Model. Chapter 12 will have other applications of the Model. By considering the 6 dimensions, our contracting will be more holistic and complete.

At the **Team Dimension** there are three contracting tools that every team can use:

1. ***Norm Setting***: This activity requires that every team member participate in naming, defining, and committing to the team's norms (behaviors and rules of engagement). This usually takes 60 to 90 minutes and defines the culture of the team. If this is the senior leadership team of a company or enterprise this will also have a dramatic influence on the company culture.

2. ***Team / Leader Contracting***: This activity focuses on clearly establishing what the leader needs and wants from the team and is prepared to offer the team. Conversely, the leader listens to what the team needs and wants from him, and what the team is prepared to offer the team leader for the entire team to be successful.

3. ***Role Contracting***: Lack of role clarity is considered a significant cause of ineffectiveness. This activity allows all team members to clarify, and get clear understanding of what they consider to be:
   - Their top 3-5 responsibilities.
   - Their top 3-5 priorities for the next 6 months.
   - The key activities that bring their roles to life.
   - The help they need from their teammates to be successful.

Why is contracting so important?

It's been said that when something goes wrong in life 25% of the reasons are health-related; the other 75% are due to poor contracting. We have found this true in working with teams. In our experience these three team contracting tools are seldom applied. Consequently, the results lead to frustration, lost time, poor performance, loss of trust and in some cases unnecessary departures and sabotage. Each of these processes takes no more than 60-90 minutes and is well worth the time investment.

Why are we so poor at contracting?

Many of us are professional procrastinators. There are several reasons (excuses) that we have encountered over the years when it comes to procrastinating 'good' contracting:

- **Don't rock the boat.** The assumption is that if we raise expectations, we may not be able to meet them, so let's keep going the way we are now. Some people in the system may get their feelings hurt if we make special concessions or agreements with others but not with them. We simply can't afford to upset people; things are going along well as they are.

- **We need more data**. The assumption is that just a bit more research or more data will allow us to make better decisions.
- **We are missing a key person.** Let's wait until this unit head or that director gets on-board, or an upcoming 'reorg' is announced. Then we will be ready to have a team contracting conversation.
- **We simply need more time.** We've encountered many leaders of teams who believe that by waiting another month or two the timing will be just right. Some leaders prefer to wait until they have been in their new role for several months.
- **We're pros; we don't need to do that.** Our implicit norms seem to be working for now.

Our general advice is the sooner the better. With few exceptions, the longer we wait the greater the ambiguity and stress we put on the team and the system. As grandmother said: "A stitch in time saves nine."

How can we facilitate contracting?

Here are three stories to illustrate the process of contracting.

Story 1: Team Leader Contracting

Several years ago, we were invited to help a corporate leadership team reach alignment on several dimensions. The team had been existing for a year without clear agreements among them on their mission, vision and strategy. In addition, they didn't have clarity on what Kathy, their team leader, expected of them or what they could expect from her. They were in desperate need of an alignment meeting.

In preparation for this workshop, we requested that every member of the team submit a question they wanted addressed during the meeting that we would then put into a survey using Survey Monkey. One of the questions on the survey was: "What should Kathy a) continue to do; b) consider starting or doing more, and c) consider stopping or doing less?" The answers were anonymous, but not confidential. The survey summary report had gone out to the entire team just one day before the 2-day workshop which was held in a beautiful chateau nestled in a wooded area outside of London.

An hour before the workshop we met with Kathy to see how she was feeling about the feedback she received in the survey. The feedback was very consistent – "you do not listen to us; you don't seem to care what we do; we don't know what you think; our meetings are a waste of time; we are not getting direction from you; you are hard to reach."

Kathy was devastated and had tears in her eyes. She said, "I need help. What will I say!? They are coming in an hour!" We said, "Kathy, this is an opportunity for you to acknowledge and thank them for the feedback. Tell them the truth – that this was devastating, hard to read, and whatever it is that you are feeling now. Speak honestly and openly with them. Perhaps you can take the next 30 minutes to get your thoughts together. We'll welcome your team as they arrive so you can show up ready to go for our 5 pm start." Kathy left the room to prepare her 'Welcome Toast.'

By 5 pm everyone had arrived. We could see by the looks on their faces that they were concerned about Kathy. We had all gathered in the beautiful lounge of this historic chateau as Kathy arrived exactly on time.

With a champagne glass in one hand and a tissue in the other Kathy forced a smile and said, "Team, this is one of the most difficult moments in my professional career. I want to thank you for being honest with your feedback. It was very hard for me to read. This is not how I want to be seen or remembered by you. And while I may disagree with some of the specifics, I want to let you know that with your help we will leave this meeting in two days having made some real changes. I am prepared to be the leader you can trust and respect. I want you to join me in a toast to this workshop and the changes we will make together." As the team members raised their glasses; there was a sense of relief and a new respect for Kathy. Everyone knew that this was a courageous step. They were ready to join her during these next two days to make these two days count.

Kathy's 'toast' set the stage for an unforgettable workshop. The second to the last session was to establish the "Team / Leader Contract" as we have already described. The Survey Summary had prepared both Kathy and her team for this session. Coming to agreement on how they would work together in the future was much easier than initially anticipated. This contracting exercise empowered both Kathy and her team. In fact, the success of the exercise led her team members to commit to conduct a similar exercise with their direct reports realizing that this would enable them to further share leadership with their own teams.

At the beginning of the closing meal on day 2, Kathy stood up and said, "Team, do you remember my initial toast two days ago?" Everyone's head nodded to the affirmative with smiles. "Well, we have experienced many amazing moments together over the last 48 hours and I want to celebrate all those moments. I could toast each one of you, but I will start by toasting just one person. Then that person will have the opportunity to toast another member of our team for one of his or her contributions during this workshop. And so on. The last lucky person gets to toast me."

And so, the Team Toasting began. At the end of dinner one of the team members raised his glass and said, "Team, what we have accomplished over the last 48 hours is truly remarkable. We simply can't go back to the way we were. Here's a toast to our future and to you, Kathy. Thank you!"

They did not 'go back'. They continued to grow and learn together. The entire organization was able to benefit by simply ensuring clear contracting across the organization. Never underestimate the power of transparency and asking for 'Help'.

Story 2: Team Member Contracting

This story takes place in Tagaytay at a picturesque hotel two hours from Manila on the crest of a semi-dormant volcano overlooking a beautiful lake with an active, yet smaller volcanic island in the middle.

We were invited to help a client's leadership team work on their business, organization and team issues. Little did we know that this beautiful setting would ignite and release some deep tensions within the team. We learned from the Managing Director that two members – the head of Sales and the head of Marketing – had not been speaking to each other directly for the previous two weeks. Therefore, the whole team was feeling the stress and was not performing at its peak. We had another contracting opportunity.

The entire organization was able to benefit by simply ensuring clear contracting across the organization. Never underestimate the power of transparency and asking for 'Help'.

After a 'kick off' with a few welcoming words from the Managing Director (MD), and a Picture / Story-Telling session we planned a 30-minute break – a bit longer than usual. However, we had a purpose. We were able to speak with the two individuals who were having a difficult time with one another. We asked these individuals if they would like some help in re-connecting and contracting with one another; they both said "Yes". After lunch, we met with the two of them in a private room. We asked each of them to prepare two lists: one of offers and one of requests they wanted to share with the other. When we got together, both were prepared with what they needed to work effectively.

Within thirty minutes they were able to meet and share their requests and offers and agreed to almost everything the other had offered or requested. Our job was very simple: provide a process and create a safe space for them to talk. At the end we provided a template that they could use as a simple contracting instrument to review on a periodic basis. One of them took our template and created their first draft in time for a breakfast conversation the following morning. With some minor changes it was good to go and so were they. They were relieved and energized. So was the team.

Two months later we checked with them to see how they were doing. They were pleased and delighted with the progress they had made since that tense contracting meeting in Tagaytay.

Story 3: Organizational Contracting

One of our clients is the largest Healthcare Network in the Philippines. On a recent workshop attended by the Leadership Team of the Holding Company and the Presidents of the 19 hospitals we contracted expectations in five areas: Purpose; Vision; Accountabilities; Leadership Behaviors; Commitments between the two leadership groups.

This was the first formal workshop between these two key groups. Collectively they are responsible for identifying and mobilizing the energy and synergies that will enable these 19 hospitals along with more hospitals yet to be acquired to work together, learn together and share leadership together in order to raise the level of engagement, effectiveness, efficiency, profitability and fun. Their ultimate goal is to better serve their internal and external clients – their employees, their patients, all of their families as well as their vendors, suppliers and shareholders.

They began to realize the vast responsibility of their collective power and influence as they refined and then committed to lead according to their agreed upon leadership behaviors and cascade the Purpose (Mission Statement), Vision Statement, Actual Accountabilities and Leadership Behaviors to everyone in each of their hospitals. They spent 2 days working together in small and large groups designed to ensure that everyone was heard, that everyone felt connected to every other person, that everyone believed that he or she was an integral part of the whole and could make a difference.

The culminating exercise was a 90-minute contracting activity that clarified the commitments (offers and requests) between the Holding Company's Leadership Team (the CEO and his Direct Reports) and the 19 Hospital Presidents. This exercise spelled out the concrete expectations that each group committed to the other. These commitments have been turned into practical instruments that will be revisited every 6 months to measure the level of commitment and provide specific feedback so they can adjust and learn. These commitments form the engine for the changes ahead. Realizing their vision and actual accountabilities will depend on them keeping these commitments. The fuel required by this engine is the support both groups receive from and offer to the other. Everyone has a critical role to play, including the crucial task of cascading the results of this workshop to each of their hospitals. With alignment between the CHRO and the CEO and the full backing of the board and hospital presidents they should succeed. This is transformation in action.

So What? ...... Insights:

Here are the key 'contracting' insights:

Effective contracting ......

- Turns hopes, frustrations, stress, and assumptions into agreements.
- Eliminates time wondering what others want and need.
- Enables anyone to ask for HELP and get it.
- Creates a safe working environment.
- Empowers both parties to focus on what matters most.
- Leads to increased trust ***when*** commitments are kept.
- Reduces time spent storming.
- Accelerates time spent performing.
- Makes life much more enjoyable and fun.
- Becomes a simple feedback instrument.
- Results in a sustainable force for change.

CHAPTER 6

The Discipline of Collect

"If you want to build a ship, don't drum up people to collect wood and don't assign them tasks and work, but rather teach them to long for the endless immensity of the sea."

Antoine de Saint-Exupery
French Author

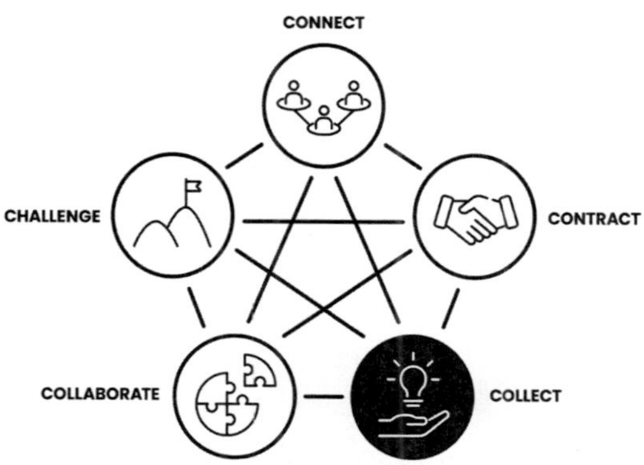

Figure 6-1: Collect

As this quote implies the real purpose of collecting is to include and inspire. Of course, you still need to collect the wood. Without the wood the ship is just a good idea.

What does the Discipline of *Collect* mean?

The discipline of ***Collect*** is to proactively seek the facts, thoughts, feelings and energy as well as the collective wisdom and intelligence, from everyone who has a stake. We need to hear their voice. This discipline is based upon a key assumption that neither the leader, nor anyone else, has all the answers. The practice of ***Collect*** requires the leader to actively reach out, invite and involve team members in conversation, with the intent of getting smarter, creating their stronger buy-in and commitment to the eventual decision to commit. ***Collect*** enables all to venture outside the confines of the leader and the team members' existing mental models, to learn and co-create new insights and ideas – even new destinations. To ***Collect*** is to be curious and complete.

The discipline of Collect is to proactively seek the facts, thoughts, feelings and energy as well as the collective wisdom and intelligence, from everyone who has a stake.

Why is Collecting significant?

Collecting leads to collaboration which, in turn, leads to greater performance and ultimately greater team satisfaction. We all have a need to contribute and make a difference – to add value. Engagement research indicates that those who contribute more have a greater feeling of commitment and ownership. Below are three stories illustrating ways leaders can collect more and better ideas that lead to increased engagement and commitment.

How can collecting be effectively accomplished?

Collecting is a great way to learn. Team coaches must have simple yet powerful tools while working with individuals and teams to collect their thoughts and feelings. The following stories describe how our Shared Leadership Coaches did just this.

Story 1: Vision in Vézelay

Nestled on a hill, in north central France near Burgundy, is a picturesque medieval town called Vézelay. The centerpiece of this town, a UNESCO World Heritage site, is an 11th century Romanesque Basilica. At the bottom of the hill stands l'Espérance, a 3-star Michelin restaurant hotel.

LIM had been invited to design and deliver a global leadership development program for the chocolate division of a large multinational with its headquarters in the USA. Twenty-four senior leaders from around the world had been selected to participate in this program. They met four times in different locations over an eight-month period, one week per module. The meeting in l'Espérance was our setting for Module 2. The program called for the participants to work as a large group of 24, and in 4 mixed teams of 6 participants per team, each one with an assigned Shared Leadership Coach. Each team worked on a different business challenge selected by the organization's senior leadership team. Each challenge had to meet several criteria: it was a current and critical issue; it required time and research to resolve; its solution had significant earnings or savings potential; it provided each team member the opportunity to learn more about himself, his colleagues, his internal client, the company, France, shared leadership and teamwork.

Four LIM coaches served as faculty for this program, and, over the 4 modules, each coach worked with each of the four teams. One day, one of the four coaches invited his team during the team breakout session to brainstorm to collect ideas on how to resolve their team challenge.

A participant in this team and an introvert made a request: "Coach, before we brainstorm, could we each spend 10 minutes writing our ideas on a flipchart, and then we can walk around and see what each of us has written?" The coach thought that was a novel request and suggested they try it out. Ten minutes later, the six participants walked from one flip chart to the next and heard the author of each flip chart read out his ideas. Once they had completed the exchange, they each took 3 more minutes to add new ideas to their flip charts that had been stimulated by what they had heard and read. They realized that they had collectively created well over 100 ideas within a period of 10 minutes – many times more than they would have in a normal brainstorming session. They were amazed with the results! The coach observed what had just happened and announced to the participant who had come up with the idea, "Congratulations, your vision has just given birth to a new tool." LIM has since refined this process and named it: ***Stop Reflect Write Report (SRWR)***.

Today we use ***SRWR*** to ensure that every participant has equal time to speak up. It gives introverts time to think which they need before they feel comfortable speaking up. It provides extroverts time to edit and clarify all their free-flowing thoughts. The real magic occurs during the writing. When introverts and extroverts start writing, one idea flows naturally to the next. Time is multiplied; ten minutes in the scenario above in effect resulted in capturing 60 minutes of insights, since each of the 6 participants had time to think. In this way, any team can generate more, and often better, ideas because they are taking time to think. Since everyone has equal opportunity to participate, the outcome is shared by every member of the team. There is an increase in commitment, engagement and sense of ownership. Teams are happier with the results. This process can be used virtually in the chat box, face-to-face using post-its, or on flipcharts. ***SRWR*** has become one of many simple yet practical tools we use with teams to help them expand their insights and collect their wisdom.

From time to time, we have been challenged by senior leaders who have said, "Look, time is money; we don't have the luxury of taking time to reflect; can't we just start talking?" Our response is simple, "Do you consider thinking an important skill for every team member?" The answer is always "Yes." And once they discover the power of ***SRWR*** there is no turning back. Thinking is important work. Collecting everyone's thoughts, feelings and energy is imperative if you want engagement, commitment, and increased performance.

Collecting everyone's thoughts, feelings and energy is imperative if you want engagement, commitment, and increased performance.

On a lighter note, our global assignments have exposed us to the importance of collecting information about differing cultural norms. The local restaurant staff for the French meeting were horrified when we requested that lunch be served in just one hour! And in Spain, when we were coaching a Netherlands leadership team, we had to delicately negotiate dinner times. The Spanish, who typically eat dinner no earlier than 9:00 pm, were adamant that this time was the correct hour to dine. We had to explain that the Dutch, who, their leader told us, usually fall down in a faint if they don't eat dinner by 6:30 pm, wanted to change the arrangement. Eventually we managed to negotiate a settlement by which the Spanish would permit dinner to be served at 7:30 pm but that the company would have to pay overtime to the kitchen staff who had to change their work schedule! Many paradigms are explored and shift during these global meetings.

Story 2: Swiss Collection

A few years ago, we had the privilege of working with a virtual team whose home base was outside of Zurich. The Managing Director had indicated that his team had several needs and spelled them out. We indicated that it it would be great to collect the thoughts of his team members in addition to his own. We asked him if we could have an hour's conversation with every member of his team to hear what they thought were the team's challenges and needs. "Great idea. Why not!" was his reply.

We used two strategies to collect their thoughts: 1) a one-on-one conversation (not an interview; we've discovered that the word 'interview' sets up formal expectations that prevent what we are hoping for – connections and candor) with every member of his team to get to know them, their concerns and advice; 2) a survey constructed by us using their questions. We used ready-made team surveys in the past but have found over the years that the teams themselves know exactly what questions they should address. So, we invited every team member to submit one question that they thought would be important to address during our 2-day face-to-face workshop. We received a very revealing list of questions that named the 'hot' topics this team was facing. We, their coaches, organized their questions with minor editing, added a few missing questions we thought would be important, and put them into Survey Monkey.

We then asked the team to complete the survey a week before our workshop. We promised all answers would be shared, but that no one would know who wrote what. We received responses from everyone and put a summary together, juggling the responses to enhance anonymity. Everyone received the report (their answers to their questions) so they could read and reflect on their collective wisdom a few days before the off-site meeting.

This survey had two significant results. It gave us a great picture of what was going on inside the team and provided the team a view of what their team colleagues were thinking and feeling. By the time the team showed up at the meeting, the meeting had, in fact, already begun. Not only had everyone read the report and was eager to address the key issues, but they were proud that their voice was going to influence their workshop, first with their questions and second with their answers.

We all met at a hotel on Lake Lucerne for an intense and engaging 2 days. During the workshop as part of the design we allocated an hour for what we call an ***R&D (Reflection and Dialogue)*** session, during which the team was able to extract meaning from the survey report. ***R&D*** is a tool to allow everyone to speak up, share opinions and insights. It is a time to listen, suspend judgments, letting everyone finish their thoughts and build upon what others were saying. It is not a debate. At the end of the dialogue the team was able to better appreciate what each other was thinking and feeling. It was not a competition for the best ideas, but a collection of good ideas. They were learning with and from one another - not telling one another what was right or what was best. By collecting their questions and their answers, they were able to discover and acknowledge the issues essential to their team's success.

This collective strategy brings three Action Reflection Learning (ARL®) principles to life: 1) Relevance – the questions and answers were theirs; 2) Tacit Knowledge – it was their questions, answers and meaning that served as the foundation for new solutions; 3) Social Learning – through conversations with us and dialogue among themselves they were able to collectively come up with insights leading to solutions to their initial questions. More on the ARL® principles will be discussed in Chapter 9.

As team coaches we simply provided the right tools at the right time for the team to use. By the end of the workshop, they had taken many decisions related to team norms, team / leader expectations, business strategy, and organizational alignment with other connected functions. Their ideas from the survey and R&D session served as the reservoir for present and future conversations.

Story 3: Gallery Walk

This story begins in Hua Hin, a picturesque sea-side village, two hours west of Bangkok. A few years ago, one of LIM's coaches was invited to work with the senior leadership team of a fast-growing entrepreneurial start up – creating a community inside Bangkok complete with hotels, restaurants, office towers, shopping plaza and a park. At the end of this workshop the leadership team decided the next step would be to bring together the entire organization so they could cascade the concepts and tools they had learned in Hua Hin to each of their functional teams. In addition, they wanted these teams to connect across their functional boundaries, and to create *Legacy Projects* that would build a stronger sense of purpose and commitment – not only for the company and their project but for the greater Bangkok community. The strategy was to tap into the collective creativity of all employees and identify *Legacy Projects*, the impact of which would live for years to come.

As team coaches we simply provided the right tools at the right time for the team to use.

Four months later, the Managing Director (MD), her six functional heads and the regional Organizational Development (OD) leader met with all 100 employees of the company in Bangkok for a 2-day workshop in one of Bangkok's fine hotels. The size of the gathering required LIM to bring 7 Shared Leadership Coaches to partner with the MD and her leadership team in their ambitious agenda: 1) build a greater sense of teamwork within and across the 6 functions; 2) introduce and practice shared leadership behaviors; 3) define and create *Legacy Projects*; 4) develop pride, ownership, and commitment. LIM's coaches came from Singapore, Vietnam, the Philippines, China, Thailand, Malaysia and the USA – providing a real cross-cultural model for shared leadership and collaboration.

The first morning was set aside for the 6 functional teams to connect at a deeper level, and to contract team norms and team /

leader expectations. Teams were spread out around the ball room into comfortable circles working with their team leaders and with each team supported by a Shared Leadership coach. The morning set the foundation for the cross-functional exchange.

The afternoon was designed to maximize diversity of experience and thought. Using a Modified Open Space process, participants self-organized into cross-functional teams to create compelling legacy dreams and plans. The MD's opening remarks set the tone: "Building a legacy is for all people and all ages. It is a powerful catalyst for personal and social change. Legacy is about living an intentional life. It is about learning from the past, living in the present and building from a future vision. We are all building a legacy every day whether we know it or not. By being intentional and working together we will increase our impact and have more fun. By this time tomorrow we will have turned our 'legacy dreams' into 'legacy projects.' Today, we will dream. Tomorrow morning, we will plan. In the days and weeks ahead, we will bring these plans to life. Now, let's dream!"

And they did. We quickly explained the process, and within 30 minutes we had established 12 Legacy Project Teams – each team focused on a different legacy dream using three simple criteria:

- The dreams (ideas) were something that would benefit the citizens of Bangkok.
- Each team must be cross-functional and be no larger than 10 members.
- Each member needed to be passionate about the idea.

For this activity, each team appointed a team facilitator who was responsible for helping each team share the work. Each team received a flipchart, post-its, tape and 10 multi-colored markers. Each flip chart was equally spaced around the ballroom walls like hours on a large clock. On each flip chart was the short title of one of the legacy dreams placed in the center of the page. Around the title were the questions: WHY? (upper right); WHAT? (lower right); HOW? (lower left) and SO WHAT? (upper left) using Bernice McCarthy's ***4MAT*** (see chapter 9).

Each legacy team had 10 minutes to collect answers from every member answering the 4 questions with drawings or post-its only — no words allowed — and without talking. After this silent collection of ideas, each team leader facilitated a quick conversation from his team to put words to the drawings and post-its. One member of each team, the storyteller, volunteered to capture the words that would ultimately be the Legacy Story.

Then, to underscore the value of the collecting process, we facilitated a Gallery Walk. Each team moved clockwise to the next poster except for one member who served as the 'team docent' or storyteller. The team docent stayed behind to brief each visiting team on the legacy picture and the story his team had created. He then invited the visitors to add their ideas using post-its or drawings telling him what they had added so he knew the meaning behind each additional contribution. Two hours passed quickly as teams moved from poster to poster every 5 minutes at the sound of a whistle. Every team had a chance to hear and contribute to all 12 dreams. After a break, each team sat around its poster while their docent provided a summary of what the others had contributed during the Gallery Walk. The 12 docents took their collection of ideas and organized them into 12 short scenarios that incorporated the ideas and insights from the entire group.

The next morning the teams had 90 minutes to begin their planning process - to putting the finishing touches to their posters and their stories along with a few concrete steps they would take to bring their legacy projects to life. A support team took photos of each poster, each team and added music in preparation for the final presentation.

One of the coaches facilitated a 36-minute *Legacy Project* presentation. Every storyteller had 3 minutes to tell his team's story projected onto the screen. In conclusion one of the coaches shared a short video called 'Lead India: The Tree' symbolizing the power of how one individual can make a big difference by standing up, speaking up, and collecting the ideas and energy of others. You can google 'Lead India-The Tree' and find the video. Their own final video of the process with music said it all. In this video they captured the key decisions and next steps while providing the positive spirit that was in the room.

The MD's closing words put everything into perspective: "Never underestimate the power of what a few individuals can do. What we have created yesterday and today will be our legacy for Bangkok. Now let's bring these dreams to life!"

Of course, a key goal of this workshop was to collect great ideas, but more importantly the workshop demonstrated powerful, visible and practical evidence of Shared Leadership coming to life under with the inspiration of the MD and her leadership team. In addition to the MD, her team and the LIM coaches, another 36 individuals – the three individuals from each Legacy Team, assumed very important roles: facilitator; storyteller; docent. Others supported the work by keeping time and organizing the final video. Shared Leadership came to life for everyone to see.

So What? ... Insights:

Effective collecting......

- Creates more and often better ideas.
- Provides a channel for passion and creativity.
- Expands time while allowing introverts to think and extroverts edit.
- Leads to consensus, ownership, and commitment.
- Can change hearts and minds and leads to transformational change.

- Gives everyone a sense of belonging, contributing, and making a difference.
- Is engaging, easy and fun.
- Increases the insights and learning for everyone.
- Transforms meetings into different kinds of engaging conversations.
- Ensures that everyone's voice is heard.

Collecting can also take place in the following settings:

- Any meeting. Invite participants in any meeting or webinar to take a minute and write down their reflections or questions on post its or put in chat.
- Social Media. You can use a similar process in email or any social media platform.
- Family dinners can become an easy way to collect insights from everyone sitting around the table.
- Many of the other processes that we have earlier introduced (R&D, Check In, OurStory, Surveys) have an inherent 'collection' step – ***SRWR***. Try it today and discover its power.

The Discipline of Collaborate

"Never underestimate the power of a few to make a big difference.
In fact, it seldom happens any other way."

Margaret Meade
American Anthropologist

What does the Discipline of *Collaborate* entail?

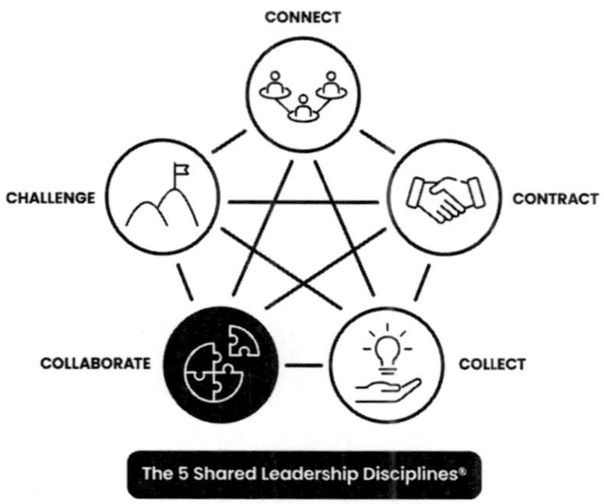

Figure 7-1: Collaborate

The Discipline of ***Collaborate*** is hugely important as our planet faces multiple divisions resulting from increased nationalistic political posturing, the scourge of Covid-19, conflicts and sustainability challenges that will determine our future as a people. Collaboration combines the science of planning and decision-making and the art of working with both friends, foes, family members and competitors. As organizations in the private and public sectors deal with uncertainty, teams and task forces must rely on key collaborative tools and processes to achieve their dreams and get work done. To ***Collaborate*** is to invite and co-create, and the world must work face-to-face and virtually to collaborate with anyone, anytime, anywhere.

Why does collaborating require reinforcement as a discipline?

Team leaders—and members — usually just assume that because they are all working on one assignment, everyone is aligned, and that there is no need to ensure that they are indeed in agreement. We would simply like to cite potential obstacles that are easily addressed by emphasizing collaboration.

To Collaborate is to invite and co-create, and the world must work face-to-face and virtually to collaborate with anyone, anytime, anywhere.

- Cross-functional biases exist and there can be a tendency for members to favor what might be advantageous to their present function rather than to the broader organizational goals
- Global organizations in particular can experience national or regional loyalties that can negatively impact a global strategy
- Changes to the Office vs Home work arrangements caused by the pandemic can have significant bearing on team cohesion and collaboration

How can organizations accentuate collaboration?

LIM uses 3 processes that we have found accentuate collaboration. They all involve meetings. A universal comment from our clients around the world is that meetings are often their least favorite, and often their least effective, work experience. Leaders, according to a 2019 Harvard Business Review study, spent 72% of their time in meetings. We are determined to make every meeting no matter what the size – virtual or face-to-face – collaborative, memorable, enjoyable and productive.

This is what you might observe if you were to 'drop in' on a team meeting that is effectively collaborating.

Everyone arrives on time and ready for the meeting to begin. If someone knows in advance that he will be late, he will notify the meeting manager and other team members. However, if a team member, for whatever reason, comes late or is not ready, another team member will welcome him with a smile, without judgment, check to see if he is okay and bring him quickly up to speed. This simple step of 'inclusion' is often neglected in meetings. As a result, the person who arrives late often feels, or is made to feel, guilty. The impact is that this person and his input are marginalized. What a loss - when a welcome smile and quick summary can encourage him to fully participate.

The agenda has been carefully thought through by the meeting manager with input solicited from every team member. Every agenda item has an outcome, an appropriate process, a lead person designated for each item, and a time estimate for that item on the agenda. Members are prepared.

The meeting begins with a few minutes allocated for team members to 'check in' and connect at a personal dimension. This is an important part of the 'work' of the team as we described earlier.

The process builds a bond of understanding, appreciation and respect among the team members and leads to a culture of care.

Key roles (meeting manager, note-taker, timekeeper) have been clearly defined and agreed upon in advance by the meeting manager. Some teams appoint a team coach to ensure the team is utilizing a good process for every part of the meeting. Most likely they rotate these roles so everyone on the team gets practice playing these important roles. This will not only make the team stronger and develop 'bench strength', but build the competence and confidence so each team member can cascade a culture of effective meetings and fruitful collaboration to his part of the organization.

The team adheres to team norms that they created and defined in a previous meeting. Everyone assumes 100% responsibility for the success of the team by making appropriate offers or requests. They also utilize agreed upon planning and decision-making processes that include everyone as they smoothly move from one agenda item to the next. Reflective moments of silence are part of the meeting process; introverts are given quiet time to think, and extroverts use that time to edit before speaking. In virtual meetings the team members use Chat to collect their inputs. This leads to better thinking, better listening and everyone having an equal opportunity to contribute. Different team members periodically summarize and paraphrase to ensure common understanding.

You will seldom, if ever, hear team members complain or blame others. In fact, if you were to observe this team for just one meeting you might not even know who the formal team leader is because the team is so comfortable and effective in sharing leadership. Learning is a part of the collaborative culture as well, and to ensure this, a debrief is scheduled at the end of every meeting. This is to align on next steps, exchange insights, and pluses and deltas that occurred during the meeting. As a result, each subsequent meeting becomes more efficient, effective and fun.

To reinforce learning, every team member has a Learning Partner. They periodically meet to exchange feedback regarding specific behaviors that each is committed to improve. Feedback is offered and received as a gift. Appreciation and true enjoyment prevail. Of course, from time to time, disagreements and conflicts arise. However, the team has processes for turning difficult conversations into learning conversations. They know what makes a difficult conversation difficult and have a process for giving feedback. They have a rich vocabulary for different types of feelings that makes expressing feelings and learning easier.

Challenges are welcomed and considered part of the creative consensus-building process. They are not taken personally. Instead, challenges are well-received as part of the learning culture. Curiosity has replaced certainty; collaboration has replaced competition. No one is shy to ask for help. In fact, meetings focus much more on supporting, making meaning and problem solving than on reporting.

Commitments are clear and documented; team members state what they will do, and by when, at the end of every meeting. Consequently, they build trust among themselves. Confidence and humility go hand in hand. Smiles and laughter abound. The team performs at a high level because members are curious and caring. They are more interested in contributing than in getting the credit.

Between team meetings, team members huddle virtually or face-to-face in twos and threes to follow up on commitments, to make requests and offers of support. They frequently solicit input from members of their respective teams thus creating a cross-functional culture of 'learning while earning.'

Team members actively replicate similar behaviors in their own teams thus cascading a shared leadership culture of collaboration across the organization. When team members are given an opportunity to increase their influence, power, and ownership, they respond by showing up fully engaged and committed. They show up because they want to, not because they have to. They proactively speak up and step up to take on critical projects.

We see similar behavior in a flock of geese. They support one another. When one goose gets tired another goose 'steps' in and takes the lead role. They look out for each other as well. When one goose gets sick or injured two others fly with the sick or injured goose to safety and then nurse it back to health before rejoining another flock. By sharing leadership, geese can increase their performance by 70%. If they can, we can.

Figure 7-1: Geese flying

Another powerful metaphor for joyful collaboration is that of a highly accomplished jazz ensemble. Each person listens and feels when the moment is right to play. Notice it's not called 'work'. They co-create a masterpiece that none of them could individually even imagine. They surprise themselves while delighting their audience. They don't just hit notes; they make music. And so do effective teams. They create, they deliver, they no longer 'execute' – a very deadly word. They bring good things to life.

We recommend three specific 'collaborative tools' that help teams or groups of two or more make their meetings magic. For the first two we will provide a short synopsis. The last one we have described in more detail as it can revolutionize team meetings and possibly transform the lives of some team members.

1. Meeting Management: W6 + H

This tool helps meeting managers design and turn every meeting into an engaging learning intervention.

- **Who?** (Attendees)
- **Why?** (Purpose, rationale and outcomes)
- **What?** (The kind of meeting)
- **When?** (Date, time and duration)
- **Where?** (Exact location – address, room, internet link)
- **Whose?** (Organizer / facilitator)
- **How?** (Agenda; roles; resources; logistics; pre-read; time for each agenda item; plan B; debrief)

2. Power Planning Process

Most meetings are less than powerful because they simply have not been well planned. We suggest that teams adopt a structured planning process to ensure that every item on their meeting agenda is linked to a specific step in the planning process. Such a planning process makes designing a meeting both easy and effective. It will also enable the meeting manager and team members to be disciplined in both preparation and delivery. It will help everyone to better keep to the topic and mind the time. It should eliminate such comments as –

- "We've already done this, haven't we?"
- "What are we supposed to do with this topic?"
- "Shouldn't we be talking about something else?"

With a structured planning process, any meeting manager can organize meetings that bring discipline, greater engagement, and power to every team in every meeting.

3. Peer Learning Process (PLP)

LIM's ***Peer Learning Process*** is designed to enable anyone to ask for help and get it in an effective, efficient and respectful way. Asking and offering help is one of the ways that will improve our connections. We all need and want help, and this is an easy way to get it – in every dimension – personal, professional, team, organization, business, and sustainability. Unfortunately, most of us have been acculturated to strive for independence and stand on our own two feet. Only later in life, and sometimes too late, do we realize that interdependence should be our goal. People need one another. We are all connected, and we are discovering this daily. We need to reach out and ask for help when we need it and offer help when we see others who need help but don't know how to ask for it.

A few years ago, one of our coaches took a weekend in the Philippines to go for a dive to see whale sharks. He was sitting under a cabana outside on the beach having breakfast when a woman happened to walk by and said, 'Do you mind if I disturb you for a minute?' His immediate facetious response was 'Yes'. She politely apologized and continued to walk away. He quickly called out and said, 'I was joking, please come back and tell me what's on your mind.' She returned and asked him if he was a diver and interested in seeing whale sharks. He told her that's why he was here and invited her to sit down and tell him more. She said that she worked at the Fun Dive Shop, and they were booking dives for later that day. He shared that he had already booked a dive via the internet with the Fun Dive Shop and was planning to go there right after breakfast.

We need to reach out and ask for help when we need it and offer help when we see others who need help but don't know how to ask for it.

Then he mentioned that she had a great job – walking down the beach finding divers to see whale sharks. Tears came to her eyes, and she began to cry. The coach asked her what was wrong. She told him that this was not her dream. She wanted to become a teacher but because of a thyroid condition she was unable to go into teaching and had to take this job to pay for the family's needs even though it didn't pay very well. In fact, she admitted that she was very depressed and had considered committing suicide the week before. Her husband and kids had no idea how depressed she was. The coach asked her if she had 30 minutes and offered her help. She said 'yes'.

Then the coach took her through the simple PLP steps that enabled her to identify questions and potential solutions.

At the end of this session a huge smile replaced her tears. She now had many helpful questions and several offers and next steps that she could act upon immediately, including confiding how she felt with her husband. To make a long story short the coach went diving that afternoon but didn't see any whale sharks, so he came back a few months later. On the second trip he met with the same woman and her husband and over dinner they had another round of PLP. Her husband had his own challenge so the three of them applied the PLP. Both received support. Now this woman is enrolled into a teaching program at a local teacher's college. She is ecstatic and well on her way to achieving her dream – becoming a teacher.

This is a collaborating tool that we have used with family, friends, colleagues, clients, and strangers. There are no limits; we all need help. We as Shared Leadership Coaches use it on a regular basis. It can be used virtually as well as face-to-face. We strongly recommend that business teams do less reporting and more supporting by using the Peer Learning Process. When this happens everyone benefits – the person with the challenge as well as the team members who are able to add value to their colleagues. Often the challenge of one is, has or will be the challenge of the others. Increased empathy and trust are two valuable off-shoots of the PLP.

A Story: Cross-Functional Collaboration

Here's a story that illustrates how two key organizational functions were able to move from almost parting to partnering.

A few years ago, we were invited to help the Medical Affairs and the Commercial leadership teams of a pharma client in Asia 're-contract' how they would collaborate. They had just introduced a high potential drug into the global marketplace and the Commercial Team was eager to sell it. The Medical Affairs Team, which was responsible for making sure the drug was introduced into the market in the right way, was by job nature more cautious, and less confident that the Commercial Team was ready to sell the drug. Further, HQ had just come out with new compliance 'ground rules' that Medical Affairs was responsible for enforcing. As a consequence, the two functions were both frustrated. The Medical Affairs Team was characterized as 'policemen' who were stopping a good thing from happening. The Commercial Team was characterized as 'cowboys' – cutting corners and only concerned with short-term profits and their bonuses. Frustration was high and collaboration was low.

We strongly recommend that business teams do less reporting and more supporting by using the Peer Learning Process.

We were invited to help the two functions overcome hurdles and to determine how to work together. Our approach included having one-on-one conversations with all the key stakeholders from the global, regional, and local levels. We co-designed a 2-day intervention with the following individuals – the global head of Medical Affairs, the regional head of Commercial, their local direct reports, plus the functional head of HR across the region and his local direct report. In addition to our face-to-face and Zoom meetings, we preliminarily organized a private dinner with the two most senior leaders to ensure that they were aligned and were willing to encourage their respective teams to be collaborative, proactive, and open to make offers and requests to each other. This dinner was key. It allowed the coaches to support these two team leaders as they spoke frankly with one another. It became clear that the attitudes and behaviors of their respective teams had, to a high degree, been a reflection of how the two leaders had been treating each other. Once the leaders were aligned in spirit, as well as word, our workshop had a greater chance of success. As grandmother says, 'Fish swim and stink from the head first.'

The dinner 'contracting' conversation set the stage for the formal start of our workshop the next morning. Within the first 10 minutes these two formal leaders publicly and personally endorsed the workshop. Their endorsement sent a strong signal to everyone in the room – "our senior leaders are engaged, aligned and committed to helping us work together. If they are, we will."

To take advantage of the release of tension, the next part of our workshop was a 'connecting' activity where everyone had 90 seconds to introduce himself with a pre-prepared slide with 2 pictures – 1) something unique about me. This could be something I've done; some place I've been; some things I have that is most likely different from everyone else in the room and 2) a picture that illustrates one adjective that describes one aspect of me. These introductions broke the ice and were fun. Everyone's voice was heard. The stage was ready for the hard work ahead.

We felt it critical to build on the opening comments of the two leaders, and one of the coaches facilitated a fishbowl conversation between the two local functional leaders. The scenario was these three people sat in a small circle, in the middle of a much larger circle formed by their direct reports, who were listening to a conversation between the two leaders. The head of MA's task was to tell the head of Commercial why Commercial was so vital to the company, and the head of Commercial's task was to convince the head of MA why MA was so important to the company. To engage their direct reports in the process, we provided an empty chair inside as part of the

Fishbowl so members of the audience could step forward and ask questions or add to the points being made and then go back to their own chair so others could come forward. This activity promoted awareness, empathy, openness and clarity - the building blocks for a paradigm shift.

After a break we introduced R&D (Reflection and Dialogue) a communication framework we use to help a group 'make meaning' of what is happening 'now'. We invited everyone to sit in one big circle so everyone could hear and see everyone else. After a brief introduction of the R&D ground rules we invited everyone to take 3 minutes to write down in their journals the insights that they extracted from the fishbowl conversation. For the next 45 minutes the group shared freely their thoughts, feelings, hopes and insights and the implications it had for them, their function, and their company.

After lunch the two teams began to develop the strategies that they needed to define to optimize their working relationship. This they did by working in small mixed groups on specific topics and questions that had emerged during the Fishbowl and R&D sessions using Open Space. They worked in mixed groups to problem-solve together, identifying the specific tactics and behaviors that both teams would use to improve their performance across their silos.

We ended our workshop the next morning with a 'formal contracting conversation' between the two functions so ongoing collaboration would become the new norm. By then everyone had experienced the process and positive outcomes of working together. Now all they had to do was name and define and adopt those 'norms' that would enable them to continue working together. Besides agreeing on a common list of norms that they all committed to follow, the two functional leads also committed to weekly lunch meetings so they could continue to connect and monitor progress.

Collaboration and CheckUps

We will not repeat what we have already written about Connect, Contract and Collect. However, when teams have a difficult time collaborating it is most likely because they haven't taken enough time to "connect" or "contract" or "collect" ideas from all. Periodically, every team needs a ***CheckUp***.

We recommend that every 6 months a team invest in a *CheckUp* to review norms, team / leader expectations, roles, organizational fitness, business purpose, vision progress and make meaning on 'How are we doing?' On road trips most of us stop periodically to stretch our legs, put gas in the car, check the oil and water, look at the map to make sure we are not only 'making good time' but we are also going in the right direction. To maintain a high performing team, we need to do the same thing. We are all human beings. We have good intentions. And often in the process of 'speeding' to get to where we are going, we get sloppy; we don't examine the details or long-term implications. By so doing, we end up with more break downs, break ups and 'difficult' conversations than necessary. These can be avoided or minimized with a periodic team *CheckUp*.

In summary, as the purpose of any team is to collaborate within the team as well as between teams and with clients and partners, three simple tips will help any team stay in peak performance:

- Establish protocols and roles that make meetings effective, efficient, and engaging – do more supporting and less reporting
- Identify and apply practical tools for planning, deciding, learning, collaborating, and making meaning
- Plan periodic CheckUps to ensure your team is focused, going in the right direction, and still having fun.

So What? ...... Insights

So, what are the key insights into the Discipline of Collaborate? Effective collaborating......

- Is critical to team productivity and organizational success
- Is an integral part of Shared Leadership
- Is the responsibility of every organizational member
- Must be part of every meeting and interaction
- Can be easy to achieve in solving problems
- Taps into our basic instincts of helping one another
- Leads to functional and cross-functional alignment
- Can save and earn millions
- Is fun
- Requires a periodic CheckUp
- Brings this saying to life – ***"Thank God It's Today"*** (instead of Thank God It's Friday)

The Discipline of Challenge

"Even when life challenges us,
it's a gift beyond all measure"

Parker Palmer
American Author

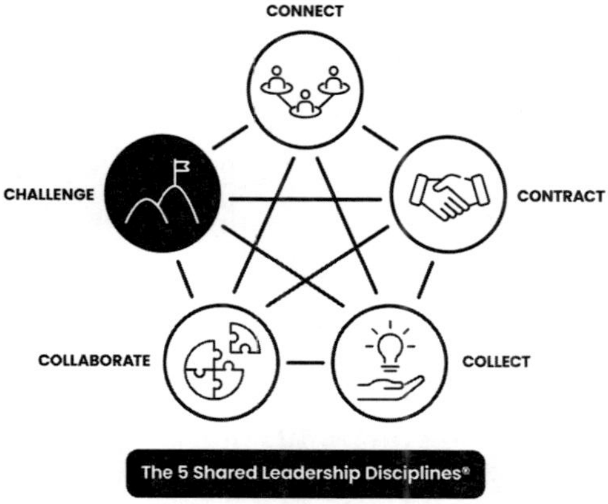

Figure 8-1: Challenge

As leaders and coaches, it is essential for us to challenge ourselves, our peers, our superiors, our direct reports and our teams to look beyond familiar ways of conducting business, to constantly consider new strategies and to consider innovative ways of addressing current obstacles. We as coaches must likewise consider how we can be more creative, how we can stretch our own approaches to develop human potential – our own, our colleagues and our clients. The concept of ***challenge*** is just as valid for leaders as well as for coaches. In any team the leader as well as team members must be willing to constantly challenge the status quo. A healthy team leads to more innovation.

What is the Discipline of *Challenge*?

It is the discipline of constantly questioning the status quo, pushing the envelope, encouraging new thinking, so as to get ahead and stay ahead.

Why is this discipline so important?

Without it, leaders, teams and organizations run the risk of becoming complacent and comfortable with just maintaining the status quo. Designs, inventions, intellectual property and our creations quickly become obsolete. Consequently, organizations lose their edge and go out of business. When learning and innovation stop, earning and productivity soon follow. Recent history reminds us of this fact. Here are just a few examples of US companies that became complacent, did not challenge themselves, who were happy with maintaining the status quo, and that now no longer exist: Polaroid; Toys R Us; Borders Books; Tower Records; RadioShack ... and the list goes on. Leaders and coaches face the same challenge. We must innovate or exit.

It is the discipline of constantly questioning the status quo, pushing the envelope, encouraging new thinking, so as to get ahead and stay ahead.

How can teams use the Discipline of *Challenge* to grow?

The process of ***challenge*** creates opportunities for individuals and organizations to develop innovative solutions to existing problems, but also to envision new prospects for growth. The purpose of challenging the current situation is not to denigrate what others have done before, or to cause them to lose face. It is not challenging for the sake of challenging. It is to strive to become better; to improve one's situation; to seek new, better ways of living; to develop new products, and more effective services for our customers. Without change we risk loss of market position, and worse, atrophy. The will to challenge and to be challenged requires openness to feedback and to maintaining a learner's mindset. Productive challenges should create a 'win / win / win / win' for me, for us, for them and for it – whatever the "it" is.

The will to challenge and to be challenged requires openness to feedback and to maintaining a learner's mindset.

In this chapter we will examine 'Challenge' from these four perspectives:

1. Me - a team leader or a coach
2. We - a business team or team of coaches working together
3. They - the client (internal or external)
4. It - the work (job, tasks, issues or solutions)

Here are five stories to illustrate these four aspects of challenge.

Story 1: Shanghai Surprise

Several years ago, LIM received a request from one of our global pharma clients in Shanghai that presented us with a wonderful challenge, one which gave us the opportunity to develop and propose a unique solution. The original request was for us to design and deliver two separate interventions. The first was aimed at instilling the organization's defined set of professional and personal leadership skills in 30 High Potential Leaders (HiPos) across China. The second was to develop the necessary skill sets of 8 Human Resources Business Partners (HRBPs) who could then cascade these same organizational leadership behaviors and skills throughout the next levels of future leaders.

We saw the chance for a novel solution that combined the two requests. Not only would this program be more cost efficient, but it would also produce quicker results and ensure a higher level of organizational effectiveness.

To achieve this, we developed a design that combined two of our major programs into one inter-connected, blended intervention. This consisted of combining a ***TCCP*** (Team Coach Certification Program) with an ***SLDP*** (Shared Leadership Development Program). We reasoned that, instead of solely using LIM's Shared Leadership Coaches (SLCs) in each program, there would be tremendous benefit in developing the 8 HRBPs as co-coaches alongside the SLCs. We coached them as we worked together as co-coaches with the 30 HiPos. In doing this we first developed their team coaching skills and then we combined these new resources with the LIM's SLCs in the leadership development program with the 30 HiPos. LIM's SLCs worked with and supported the new internal team coaches to expand their skills as they co-coached the HiPos.

One of the pre-determined workshops in Session 2 of three face-to-face sessions was an introduction to the company's latest marketing strategy for a new product that was soon to be launched. The head of Product Marketing for this product gave a one-hour workshop on the emerging product marketing strategy.

The product manager had prepared a well-organized slide deck of approximately 30 slides. Most of these slides were packed with important charts, graphs, statistics and too many words in small print. She knew her material well, but lacking confidence, she read each slide out loud, which was distracting since most of the audience could read faster than she could speak. Four results handicapped the presentation's effectiveness: 1) she lacked expression in tone; 2) she read every slide text in a low, monotone voice; 3) she failed to make eye contact with her audience; 4) the content on each slide was so dense that even those closest to the screen were unable to read what was on each slide.

Consequently, her audience very quickly disengaged with her and just as quickly engaged with their mobiles. In fact, 22 members of the 30 **SLDP** participants were on their mobiles, while only 8 participants appeared to listen. All the coaches noticed what was happening and looked to the lead coach for guidance into what to do.

Now imagine that you are the lead Shared Leadership Coach. You are seated along with the participants and your fellow coaches. You look at your watch and see that there are 40 minutes to go in this session. In Session 1 you facilitated a 'norm-setting' workshop in which every participant had agreed that Active Listening and Being Present (not using mobiles) were two key norms that should guide the work.

[Before reading further, stop and reflect for 3 minutes and write down what you would do if you were the lead coach. Ready? Do you have your 'plan'? When you're ready continue reading.]

Here's what the lead Shared Leadership Coach did. First, he did what you just did and took 3 minutes to plan. Then he slowly walked to the front of the room where the head of marketing was speaking. When she took a pause he said, "Excuse this interruption. Since many of you have a need to check your messages, we will take an internet break for 10 minutes, so that after the break we can all give our presenter 100% of our attention. We will begin again at 11:30 and extend this session by 10 minutes, so we will delay lunch until 12:10."

During the short break, he asked the presenter if she had been aware that two thirds of the group were focusing on their mobiles. She said that she wasn't. He invited her to consider how she could bring more life into her presentation and asked her if she was interested to hear a couple of suggestions. She said, "Of course." Then he quickly offered her a couple of ideas to consider right away: "Here are two things you can try: 1) simply talk to the group rather than read your slides as the material is very detailed and impossible for the audience to read and listen to you at the same time; besides you said that you would send them your slides anyway. 2) Look at your audience; your eye contact will create a more intimate connection and encourage them to focus on you and what you are saying." He offered to meet with her in the next few days, if she was interested, to give more feedback. He suggested that she use the next 9 minutes to gather her own thoughts on what she would do. She thanked him and he took his seat.

After 10 minutes she called the group back and had a much more engaging remainder of her session. During lunch the lead coach invited the other coaches (both LIM and HRBPs) to huddle by having lunch together and shared with them why he did what he did and what he planned to do when everyone reconvened for the session after lunch. They all agreed that his intervention had been necessary, and importantly, that he had managed to help both group and the presenter without her losing face. Now it was time to extract insights from everyone.

Before the afternoon session was to begin at 1:10 the lead coach invited everyone to stand outside (as it was a beautiful day) in a tight circle so everyone could share an 'Accidental Insight', a very informal and efficient tool, to make meaning from the morning and lunch conversations. As this was a common practice after lunch everyone was looking forward to this informal exchange.

As expected, the insights focused mostly on the unscheduled 'internet break'. The exchange was full of insights and became one of the most memorable moments during the program. Some of the insights included:

- The value the coaches bring by having the courage to stand up, challenge and change the situation in the moment.
- The importance of finding the 'right' learning moment and create a win / win situation for all the parties.
- How important it is to ensure that a group / team adheres to its norms.
- The power of 'Just in Time Learning' interventions, followed by the intentional act of capturing the 'Accidental Insights' learning from among the whole group.
- The importance of a Huddle to ensure alignment among team members.
- The importance of preparing and delivering presentations that engage participants so that they are not tempted to pull out their mobiles.

Story 2: Missing in Merida

Merida, Mexico was the setting for another **SLDP** we designed for one of the market leaders in the dredging business, a firm based in the Netherlands. LIM was working with a group of 24 global leaders, mostly Dutch, based all over the world, for the first module of a four-module program.

As we usually do, we placed the participants into project teams that had real clients and addressed real business problems and opportunities within their company that could potentially earn or save the company millions of dollars. In the process, the participants discovered more about themselves, teamwork, consulting, shared leadership, and the company. To ensure that participants would deepen their insights, we had the teams self-select based one criterion - that no one worked on a project team where they might be perceived by the others as an expert. We wanted them to tap into their natural wisdom and tacit knowledge rather than tap on the shoulders of a colleague who was already working on a similar challenge or was familiar with the circumstances. To reinforce this point, we urged participants to maximize diversity when forming project teams. So, for example, a project team might consist of participants from different countries, different functions and different ages and genders while working with a client and problem separate from their country or region and areas of expertise. Therefore, the teams were able to more easily challenge the status quo, generate creative solutions and tackle systemic organizational challenges.

Day One was basically set aside for the total group to receive an overview of the overall program, connect with one another at a personal dimension, contract norms and get into their project teams to meet their colleagues and coaches.

Day Two was dedicated for the teams to meet their Senior Management clients who joined the program by video from the Netherlands. The four teams met in separate rooms to work on their assigned projects with their respective coaches. After contracting our roles as team coaches in our respective rooms, we sat apart from the team and observed the dynamics of their process. We looked for JITL (Just-In-Time-Learning) opportunities.

In one of the rooms, it didn't take very long before one of the participants turned away from his teammates and challenged his coach with a bit of frustration in his raised voice and said, "Excuse me, I'm missing something; you haven't taught me anything yet. How long do we have to wait?"

This was the JITL opportunity the team coach was looking for. He asked the others if he could join the team and respond to that question. By the way, for those of you who do not know the Dutch, as a general tendency they are not shy to voice their concerns or feelings. This is exactly the kind of behavior that the coaching faculty were hoping for.

Once the coach pulled up his chair and joined his team he turned to the individual and thanked him for speaking up and challenging him. He summarized for everyone what he took away as a three-pronged question – 'What is learning? How do I learn best? How can we, your coaches, design effective learning interventions?' He went on and said, "These are probably the most profound questions that we will address in this program." He then introduced R&D (Reflection and Dialogue) a tool that we described earlier in this book. After five minutes of reflection on the focus question the team began a very memorable dialogue. This conversation opened their eyes to multiple ways of learning based on LIM's 10 ARL principles and project-based inductive learning. The coach was able to move from a potential defensive challenge into a rich conversation where everyone, including the coach, was able to share differing perspectives and definitions of learning. One of the insights was how they as team leaders should resist becoming defensive with tough questions or different perspectives and welcome challenges from their team members as well. This dialogue was much more effective than any lecture could ever have been.

The bottom line: turn a challenge into a JITL opportunity. Resist being defensive. Welcome diverse perspectives. Be genuinely appreciative. Remember that there are many ways that people learn. We as coaches and leaders must always recognize this in our meetings, program designs, and in our conversations and interventions with team members.

As mentioned above, the Dutch are typically very direct in their comments, and this **SLDP** was composed mainly of Dutch leaders - most of whom were engineers by training. Obviously, the Dutch are as diverse as any other culture, however, there is ample evidence that shows that rational thinkers – scientists, engineers, mathematicians, auditors, financiers, accountants, etc. – tend to be more comfortable with a logical and factual approach to learning. This can lead to the expectation that learning is primarily transactional, quantified, measured, and organized. The team coach knew this and so was seeking the appropriate opportunity to provide the group with evidence that learning is also inductive, intuitive, social, systemic, integral, gradual, continual and transformative.

The key take aways were:

- **Challenges:** A challenge to any individual, team, organization, business, government or even our planet can be a powerful catalyst for learning.
- **Transactional and Transformational:** Learning can be transactional (lead to action) as well as transformational (lead to a change of attitude and behavior).
- **JITL:** Look for Just in Time Learning opportunities. These are some of the most memorable and effective.
- **Defensiveness:** Resist defensiveness; be positive and alert for new options.

Story 3: Glass Ceiling in Sweden

On the next to the last day of a four-module **SLDP** with one of our automotive clients in Sweden, the program coaches were approached by four female participants with distraught looks on their faces. The coaches asked them what was on their minds. The women confided that something important was missing in this program and were wondering if it was too late to address it. They had the coaches' attention who asked what the women had in mind.

The women reminded the coaches that they were only four women out of 24 in this global leadership program and by the sheer numbers alone they felt that the female perspective had been minimized. Since this was a male-dominant company, there was a "glass ceiling" of which only the women were fully aware. They asked the coaches if they would be willing to address this issue before the program ended. It was a challenging request that the coaches could not refuse. They agreed to redesign the agenda of the last day. Overnight the coaches changed the design thanks to these courageous women who asked for help and were willing to challenge the program staff.

Here's what happened. The lead coach opened the final session the following morning with a summary of the conversation from the night before - acknowledging the "glass ceiling" conversation and thanked the four female participants before introducing the new design of the final day.

Then he asked the women and men to get into two separate circles with enough distance between them so both the men and the women had some degree of privacy. Each person was invited to take two minutes of silence and write down one question related to the glass ceiling issue that they wanted the other gender to answer. After sharing their questions within their respective circles, each group selected four questions to ask the other group. When both groups had selected their four questions the women were asked to stand behind the circle of men and give them one question at a time to read. After a 2-minute pause to reflect, the men entered into a fishbowl dialogue – talking among themselves, without looking at the women. All four questions were handled in the same fashion. The women took notes.

After a brief break the women sat down in their circle and the men formed a circle behind them and offered their four questions one at a time using the same process. Finally, the lead coach asked everyone to sit in one circle including the coaches with the women interspersed among the men for an R&D (Reflection and Dialogue) conversation on the question: "What have I learned?" The energy was high; blame and guilt were replaced with appreciation. "Us" and "Them" was replaced by "We". The learning was rich; paradigms were beginning to crumble.

After lunch it was time to move from insight to action. We conducted a workshop where everyone was invited to submit yet another question – a question that could lead to positive action. The goal was to involve everyone to come up with a plan and next steps that would address some aspect of this inequity. Everyone was eager to break the glass ceiling.

The result of the workshop was encouraging. Participants came up with a few clear actionable recommendations that two women and two men then took to the executive team, on behalf of the entire program. The executive team (mostly men) accepted all the recommendations. They were relieved and grateful that this leadership group had accepted their challenge by coming back to them with recommendations that they (the participants) felt were necessary to make their organization better and more inclusive.

The beauty is that this combination of insights can be adapted to almost any challenge anywhere. When an intervention is relevant there is always a high probability for progress. When relevance is missing, we all need to speak up and challenge. Here are some guidelines for team leaders and team coaches:

- **Be open:** if the needs change, the design must change.
- **SRWR:** identify the urgent and important questions underlying the need.
- **Fishbowl:** create an environment where the answers to these questions can be heard.
- **Plans:** design a process where the participants decide which questions need to be converted into a plan and recommendations that lead to action.
- **Next Steps:** ensure that the plans and recommendations see the light of day with clear next steps – who will do what by when.
- **Debrief:** extract thoughts and feelings on the content and the process plus implications and applications so the process can be replicated where appropriate. This is an easy way to get feedback and feed forward.

Story 4: Moon Shot

Two LIM coaches were invited to work with the Managing Director of one of our pharma clients and his team during their annual team development workshop in January in the Philippines a few years ago. Our hotel was perched on a cliff overseeing the beautiful Balayan Bay with a spectacular view of the sunset – the perfect spot to be inspired. As usual we offered to support the leadership team on 6 dimensions: Business; Organization; Team; Professional; Personal and Sustainability.

During the design stage for the business dimension the MD wanted the team to walk away with a strategy and 100% commitment from every team member to deliver 100% of their already agreed upon financial target to the region. The year before they had missed their target by 4% for very valid reasons, however, the MD didn't want that to happen again. One of the coaches asked the MD, "Would you be interested in getting 110% of your target?" The MD replied, "Were you listening to me? Last year we were only able to get 96% of our target; I will be happy with 100%." The coach replied with a smile, "Were you listening to me - Would you be interested in going for 110% of your target?" A smile crossed the MD's face and he said, "Of course I'd like 110% of our target; I'm just being realistic."

Sometimes, as coaches we need to challenge our clients and help them to not let 'reality – often assumptions based on past experience' get in the way of a 'crazy' dream or idea. The coach suggested that they design a Moonshot Session and go for 110% of target promising it would feel more like a game than work. The MD agreed to give it a 'go'. The two coaches had no idea where the additional 10% ($8 million) might come from but trusted that the collective knowledge of the team was more than sufficient to reach that figure.

On the day of the workshop several of the participants were apprehensive of the Moonshot Session. The coaches were finally able to convince the team to treat it as a game and divided the large group into two smaller mixed groups of 6 per group. Before they broke into their separate breakout rooms, the coaches made one request of everyone: "Before you go into your separate rooms, please take 5 minutes and silently using SRWR (Stop Reflect Write Report) to write down every idea you have, as crazy as it might seem now, on where you might be able to find just a small fraction of that $8 million". After 5 minutes of silence and writing the groups went to their two separate rooms – each room with one Shared Leadership Coach.

When the two small groups came back together after an hour of exchanging ideas, they presented their results to the other team. To their joint surprise they discovered that they had actually identified a potential figure of $10 million. The MD's mouth opened wide as did most members of the team. When the team debriefed how that could happen, they agreed that much of the credit went to those 5 minutes of reflection and the SRWR. They took time to think. Too often we begin a discussion without thinking. Five minutes of thinking times 12 team members was the equivalent of 60 minutes of thinking. Thinking is real work.

The following day the coaches designed a follow up session so that there was a detailed plan to ensure that each of the individual 'pocket ideas' were translated into a solid plan with specific commitments, and with timelines and a champion for each 'pocket'. This was an uplifting experience for both the team and the coaches. It demonstrated the power of a playful challenge, allowing oneself to dream and discover what can happen when we make time to think and tap into our tacit knowledge and unleash our imagination.

The intervention we offered as coaches was simple. First, we used one of our most effective tools, SRWR, and then we coupled it with the suggestion of treating this assignment as a game. All of us have doubts which can obstruct us from achieving success; often we simply need a little push to dream and play and bring back our childlike 'why not' spirit which is what enabled us to learn so much as kids. When we as coaches, demonstrate our authenticity and our own childlike spirit, we can have a huge influence in our work with teams. In this case the suggestion by the coaches led to increased innovation, improved cross-functional collaboration and a demonstration of shared leadership. There were other results as well:

- Increased revenue.
- Improved performance.
- Increased confidence in the leadership team's own abilities.
- Increased respect across the region.
- Recognition of the power of reflection (thinking) as a method to collect ideas and wisdom that can lead to all of the above results.
- Reinforcement of the power of challenging assumptions.
- Plus, an incentive trip to Japan for three days for the entire company.

Story 5: Personal Passion Project

In one of the SLDPs we conducted for a European client we instituted what we called our "Personal Passion Project". This was in addition to the Project Team challenges that served as the arena for learning about self, team, organization, business, teamwork, shared leadership, coaching, consulting and the company. The Personal Passion Project was an opportunity for every participant to reflect and identify one small thing that might make a big difference IF someone would take the lead. The four criteria were simple:

a. There was a clear **purpose** and measurable result.
b. The individual had a real **passion** for that challenge.
c. The individual would develop a **plan** leading to a potential solution to the challenge during the program.
d. The individual had to take his/her plan to a key decision-maker.

Ted, one of the participants in this program, identified his passion project that met all four criteria. His Personal Passion Project was simply stated in his focus question: "What will I do to find a solution to boring, time-wasting meetings in our company?" On his own time, he developed a plan that required the CEO and the Senior Leadership Team (SLT) of the company to get actively involved. He presented his plan to the CEO and SLT in one of their meetings citing the estimated number of wasted hours senior managers spent in meetings with no stated purpose or agenda and the consequent loss of energy and engagement. The SLT received this initiative with enthusiasm and gratitude. They turned Ted's request into a company policy that required every meeting including their own to have a stated purpose and agenda or NO MEETING. The results were felt immediately: more effective and efficient meetings; increased focus; higher engagement and better results.

There were other benefits and learnings as well:

- Turning a challenge into an opportunity and win / win / win (Ted / SLT / all employees).
- A reminder to all of us – that a challenge can lead to positive change – all we must do is speak up.
- The power of one in leading to change.
- Anyone can share leadership.

So What? ...... Insights

In summary, the 'Challenge' lessons from these five stories are very compelling:

- Constantly challenge the status quo.
- Challenge at 4 dimensions: Me; We; Them; It.
- Any kind of challenge can be turned into a learning opportunity for the challenger and the individual(s) being

challenged. Leaders must be open to be challenged by their team members and colleagues.

- Every voice matters: request; offer; listen; acknowledge; appreciate; respond; act.
- Challenging constantly moves the needle.
- Challenging requires courage, care and humility and demands openness to a variety of perspectives.
- Challenging can be fun if you don't take yourself too seriously. It makes life interesting.
- Don't let perceived reality or culture get in the way of a dream.
- Back up a dream with an action plan and empowered champions.
- Speak up and ask for or offer HELP, a valuable 4-letter word that is not used enough. It's never too late to ask for or offer HELP.
- A few simple group processes like SRWR, Fishbowl, R&D and Personal Passion Project, can lead to solutions that can be transactional as well as transformational. Use the questions and ideas of team members to find solutions.
- Shared Leadership really works.

CHAPTER 9

The Science of Shared Leadership Disciplines®

"I have no special talent.
I am only passionately curious"

Albert Einstein
German-born physicist

In the last 5 chapters, you learned about the What, Why, How and So what of each of the 5 Shared Leadership Disciplines®. As you have noted, each of the disciplines can enable any leader, anywhere and at any level of leadership to get the full engagement of every team member, and to create the necessary environment and conditions that make it easy for team members to speak up, step up and take on more ownership and responsibility.

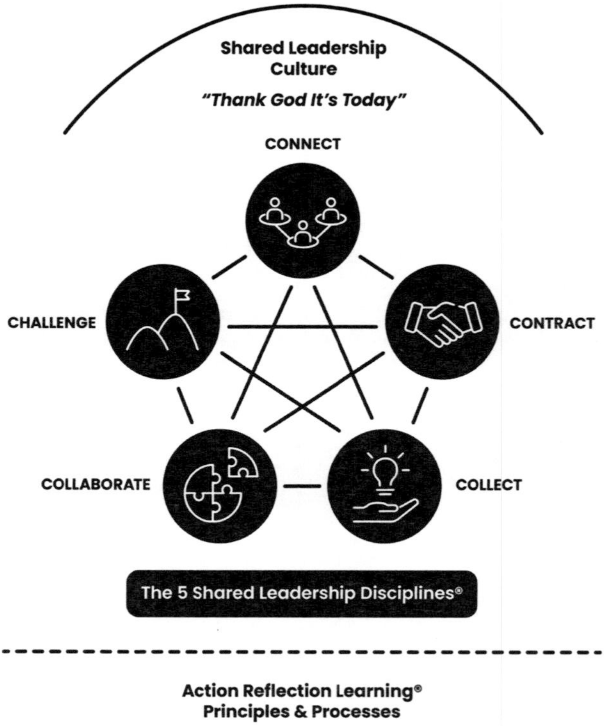

Figure 9-1: Shared Leadership Disciplines®

The key reason for the effectiveness of the Shared Leadership Disciplines® is its "learner-centric operating principles". These 5 Disciplines, and the team coaching tools, some of which are described in this book, are based on 10 Action Reflection Learning (ARL®) Principles. These principles are founded on rigorous research and serve as the foundation of the 5 Shared Leadership Disciplines®. In this chapter, we do not cover the principles in depth, but rather discuss the questions: **"What are the ARL® principles?"** and **"Why are they significant?"**

In 1986 LIM and the MiL (Management in Lund) Institute decided to change the name of their leadership development approach from Action Learning to "Action Reflection Learning". The rationale was two-fold – 1) recognize the power and role that reflection has in the learning process and 2) differentiate their action learning practice from other action learning practices that were beginning to emerge in the 1990s. Then in 2005 they accepted an offer from Isabel Rimanoczy, Boris Drizin and Paul Roberts, three academics, to interview LIM and MiL coaches to extract the common principles and practices underlying ARL. Through their extensive research, the trio posited there are 10 learning principles that make ARL effective for team learning. Experiential application of the principles has been described in detail in the following two books: 1) ***Action Reflection Learning: Solving Real Business Problems by Connecting Learning with Earning*** – co-authored by Isabel Rimanoczy and Ernie Turner; 2) ***Gentle Interventions for Team Coaching: Little things that make a BIG difference*** – authored by Ernie Turner.

We recognize and appreciate the pioneering work of these 3 researchers and, in particular, Isabel Rimanoczy, who pulled it all together.

The 10 ARL® Principles

Principle 1: Tacit Knowledge

"Knowledge exists within individuals in implicit, often unseen forms. It is frequently underutilized but can be accessed through guided introspection."

Tacit knowledge is the reservoir of skills, knowledge, experience, insights, and wisdom that every person has learned and accumulated in his life. It is often not easily expressed. The term "tacit knowing" is attributed to Michael Polanyi, a British scientist and philosopher who first used this term in his book "Personal Knowledge" (1958). His words summed it up best: "We can know more than we can tell". Socrates (470-399 BC) describes the teacher (or the leader or coach in our context) as being like a mid-wife, who brings out the wisdom that is hidden inside them.

We are typically unaware of how much we know until given a few minutes to reflect and recall the knowledge accumulated in the lockers of our minds. Collectively we are often wiser than any expert. By asking meeting participants to reflect and write down their ideas or questions related to an agenda item, we will discover a wealth of wisdom. Often in a meeting or workshop after a few minutes of 'content input', we will give our audience time to pause and take just two minutes and share an insight, question, or story pertinent to the topic. This pause provides the opportunity for participants to access, and then share their tacit knowledge so that it becomes explicit and enlightens the group.

Principle 2 : Relevance

"Learning is optimized when the focus of the learning is owned by, relevant to, important and timely for the individual or team."

The principle of ***Relevance*** is about learning that is connected to, or that can be applied to, our real world — to our actual situations, challenges or even questions in our heads. Lev Vygotsky (1896-1934), a Soviet psychologist, wrote about situational learning where individuals use their current situation as the most important area for learning. In his words, knowledge is constructed, with the interweaving of new concepts with prior concepts. Malcolm Knowles (1913-1997), an American educator, popularized the term "andragogy", meaning the art and science of adult learning. In his book, "From Pedagogy to Andragogy", one of his key insights about the adult learners is that they "become ready to learn something when they experience a need to learn it to cope more satisfyingly with real-life tasks or problems".

One easy way to establish the relevance of a topic or statement is to ***ask a question*** such as, 'What question do you want answered in this meeting or workshop?'. Another simple and effective way is to conduct a preliminary conversation or survey to discover precisely what participants want to know or do. If a meeting or workshop is not relevant to the participants, then they will simply not be engaged.

Principle 3: Reflection

"The ability to thoughtfully reflect on experience is an essential part of the learning process and enables greater meaning and learning to be derived from a given situation."

Reflection in learning is a deliberate and active process of consciously engaging our self-awareness by stepping back to recall, make sense of, and learn from current or prior experiences. John Dewey (1859-1952), an American philosopher and reformer, is said to be the Father of Reflection. In his words, "we do not learn from experience ...... we learn from reflecting on our experience". Since Dewey's initial work, various models of reflection have been developed. One such model was David Kolb's Experiential Learning Cycle (1984) where learning takes place in four stages. A person has an experience; he reflects on the activity or experience; he learns from the experience gaining understanding and insights; and lastly, he tries out and tests new skills. According to Donald Schon (1983) from Harvard University, reflection is the ability of people to "think what they are doing while they are doing it". He recognized that there are 2 types of reflection: 1) ***Reflection On Action*** where you look back and reflect after something has happened and 2) ***Reflection In Action*** where you literally reflect on your feet and decide on your next action. Since 1986, LIM has used the Action Reflection Learning cycle in our work with clients and coaches (see Figure 9-2).

Figure 9-2: Action Reflection Learning

By reflecting on what we did or said we would do, we can discover things we should repeat and the things we should start or stop. One easy practice is to allocate a few moments of reflection at the end of every meeting and invite everyone to share a few **Plusses**

(Positives) and a few **Deltas** (suggestions for improvement) that could make the next meeting even better. Before long, meetings or workshops will naturally improve if those insights are applied. Probably the easiest and most effective tool that we created is what we call ***SRWR*** (Stop Reflect Write Report). As the name implies there are 4 important steps: Stop (be silent); Reflect (think); Write (capture ideas and questions using Post-it notes, a journal or Chat box); Report (share your written thoughts with others). The results are amazing. Introverts need silence and writing to do their best thinking. Extroverts need a little quiet time although this can be very difficult for them but writing helps them edit what they want to say. By reflecting, a team creates more and better ideas or questions. People listen more attentively because most of us cannot listen and think at the same time. The result is that everyone has an equal opportunity to be heard and it becomes easier for the leader to get shared ownership. This process works like magic.

Principle 4: Self-Awareness

"Building self-awareness through helping people understand the relationship between what they feel and think, how they act, and their impact on others, is a crucial step to greater personal and professional competence."

Self-awareness is how we see ourselves in a variety of areas such as our thoughts, feelings, behaviors, values, strengths, weaknesses, our impact on others and also our understanding of how others view us. Scholars have linked self-awareness with adult development, which is portrayed as a process involving the awareness of, and the integration of, the conscious and the unconscious. John Locke's "An Essay Concerning Human Understanding" (1689) is one of the first modern conceptualizations of "consciousness", a term close to "self-awareness". Carl Jung (1875-1961) posited that "there is no cure and no improving of the world that does not begin with the individual himself". One important component of self-awareness is emotional intelligence (EI), popularized by Daniel Goleman (1995) with his four dimensions: 1) Self-Awareness; 2) Social Awareness; 3) Self-Management and 4) Relationship Management. Numerous studies have shown the correlation between high EI and performance. It is no surprise that improving self-awareness is perceived to be of high importance and value in leadership education and development.

One easy way to increase self-awareness is to ask for feedback. ***360 Feedback*** is very valuable but takes time and lots of effort. ***Fast & Focused Feedback*** takes only minutes and can allow a team of 10 people to ask and get valid feedback privately in 20 minutes. ***Learning Partners*** are also valuable in providing just in time feedback.

Principle 5: Integral

"People are a combination of mind, body, spirit, feelings and emotions, and respond best when all aspects of their being are considered, engaged, and valued."

This principle is deeply rooted in humanistic psychology, which aims to focus on the whole human being, emphasizing the individual's potential and stresses the importance of growth and self-actualization. It also suggests that all learning is emotionally grounded and that our mental models are not just cognitive constructs but are also attached to deep levels of identity and feelings. The foundations of humanistic psychology were laid by Abraham Maslow (1908-1970), Carl Rogers (1902-1987) and Charlotte Buhler (1893-1974). To this date, the humanistic branch of psychology is as valid as it was in their times.

This principle states that learning is more than mental. It needs to address the head, heart, hands, and health of an individual, team and organization. We have thoughts, feelings, intuitions and want to do something with what we are learning. ***Reflection and Dialogue*** (or R&D) and ***Story Telling*** are two of the concepts we use to bring this principle to life. The purpose of learning is to constantly challenge and shift our perspectives. This happens subtly and sometimes dramatically. Other tools to enable individuals and teams to shift their paradigms include research results, surveys, feedback, and dialogue. Probably one of the easiest and most effective tools is our ***Peer Learning Process.*** This non-threatening process is designed so that anyone can ask for help and receive it from one or more of his colleagues, teammates, friends, or family, and to do so within 30-40 minutes. This process can be transformational.

Principle 6: Social Learning

"Learning emerges through social interaction, and, therefore individuals learn more with others than by themselves."

Social learning is based on the Social Cognitive Theory (1977) developed by American psychologist, Albert Bandura, who suggested that people can learn by observing others. We are shaped by others, and we shape others in our social interactions and most human behavior is learned through the process of observing, modeling and imitating.

One of the easiest and most profound ways of learning since the beginning of time has been by sharing insights, questions, opinions, feelings, and experiences with others. Coffee breaks, breakout rooms, lunch, and dinner conversations as well as ***Walk & Talk*** can be effectively used to discover what is really going on in a group. Open Space, an informal and dynamic meeting concept, developed by Harrison Owen, is one way to self-organize a meeting into a series of coffee break-like conversations where real work can get done effectively, efficiently and with fun.

Principle 7: Systems Thinking

"We live in a complex, interconnected, co-created world. In order to better understand and tackle individual and organizational issues, we have to take into account the different systems and contexts which mutually influence one another."

This principle has its roots in systems theory. The Austrian biologist Karl Ludwig von Bertalanffy (1901-1972) posited a system theory that hypothesized that all elements of any living system were connected, creating webs of relationships. "Systems thinking deals with wholes rather than separate entities." In the behavioral sciences, this principle is present in the Gestalt psychology which stresses connectivity and inter-relatedness. In the field of learning, Peter Senge's *The Fifth Discipline* (1990) propounded systems thinking as one of the five disciplines that would enable an organization to learn.

Individuals, teams, organizations, businesses and, in fact, all living beings are inter-connected systems. We simply need to use these connections to engage and expand the learning opportunities available in every situation. The **Pentagon-Plus System Model** (see Chapter 5 & 12) is a useful framework that allows leaders to systematically consider opportunities, consequences and implications from a holistic approach by examining six different dimensions – business, organization, team, professional, personal and sustainability.

Principle 8: Facilitated Learning

"A specific role exists for an expert in methods and techniques for teaching and learning who can optimize the learning of both individuals and teams."

Learning increases when there is a person or persons providing support for the learning. Edgar Schein, former professor at the MIT Sloan School of Management and a leader in the field of organizational development, introduced the concept of "process consultant", to refer to a person who supports learning by focusing on the process by which the individual or team is carrying out the task.

A Shared Leadership Coach wears several important hats such as: 1) Co-designer of workshops and programs; 2) Observer of team interactions; 3) *Facilitator* of Just-In-Time Learning Interventions; 4) Team and individual Coach and Mentor. In each of these roles the Shared Leadership Coach utilizes the other 9 ARL principles as his guide in designing interventions and making decisions that support the team's learning. A team coach who has mastery of the ARL principles and knows how to use most, if not, all the tools in LIM's Shared Leadership Team Toolkit, will be able to help any team to share leadership and transform itself, thus making a positive impact on their organization and business.

Principle 9: Paradigm Shift

"The most significant learning occurs when individuals are able to shift the perspective by which they habitually view the world, leading to the capacity for greater understanding (of the world and of the other), self-awareness and intelligent action."

Paradigms are significant in that they shape how we perceive the world. Our mental models become the interpretative filter through which we interact with others and with the world. Kenneth Craike (1914 -1945), a Scottish philosopher and psychologist, was the first to use the term "mental model" and he posited, "our brain has small-scale models to anticipate events". Philip Johnson-Laird, an American philosopher in Princeton University, wrote on mental models, examining the mental processes that underlie our reasoning. Several theorists of organizational development, such as Chris Argyris, David Schon, Peter Senge and Jack Mezirow, have all written of the importance of uncovering our mental maps and models so as to increase awareness, learning and transformational change.

Bernice McCarthy's Learning ***4MAT*** is a simple and powerful example of how 4 different learning style preferences can enable coaches, teachers, and facilitators of learning to address each of the 4 different learning preferences: 1) Why? (purpose and reasons); 2) What? (concept and ideas); 3) How? (process and methods); 4) So What? (impact and applications). In so doing every participant has his learning preference addressed while also being exposed to

3 other equally important learning preferences – thus expanding his knowledge and appreciation of other learning preferences. Over time and practice a paradigm shift occurs and every learner becomes stronger in all 4 learning preferences.

Principle 10: Repetition and Reinforcement

"Practice brings mastery and positive reinforcement increases assimilation."

This principle is based on behavioral science. Edward Thorndike (1874-1949), an American psychologist, developed the Law of Effect which focuses on consequences. It states that "behavioral responses that were most closely followed by a satisfying result were most likely to become established patterns and to occur again in response to the same stimulus". B.F. Skinner (1904-1990), another American psychologist, developed the theory of operant conditioning where the probability of a response being repeated depends on whether that response was rewarded or punished. He introduced the term "reinforcement" which suggests that behavior which is reinforced will be strengthened, whereas behavior that is not reinforced will be weakened and diminished.

Equally importantly, the ARL® principles help to accelerate the team and individuals' learning, creating a sustainable competitive advantage when these principles are internalized and applied.

Growing wiser as we grow older doesn't just happen; it requires ***repetition and reinforcement***. Repetition and reinforcement help us to go from conscious practice to unconscious mastery. All it takes is practice, practice, and more practice — with colleagues, learning partners, clients and mentors to observe and provide feedback. Reinforcement takes place when everyone recognizes and appreciates the efforts. Action Reflection Learning is itself a powerful appreciative approach, with the leader, team and coach looking out for what has been done well and recognizing the learning that comes from new actions and practices.

So What? ...... Insights

Over the years we have witnessed that these 10 ARL® principles have enabled leaders and LIM's Shared Leadership Coaches to consciously transform any meeting, workshop, and 'training' intervention into a learning experience. Each principle comes to life when an experienced practitioner applies simple concepts, processes and tools that were either created by LIM or adapted from existing concepts and tools created by others.

This deep knowledge of the principles that define learning and the skillful application of practical concepts and tools will lead to success in developing a shared leadership mindset and a higher performing team anywhere. Equally important, the ARL® principles help to accelerate the team and individuals' learning, creating a sustainable competitive advantage when these principles are internalized and applied.

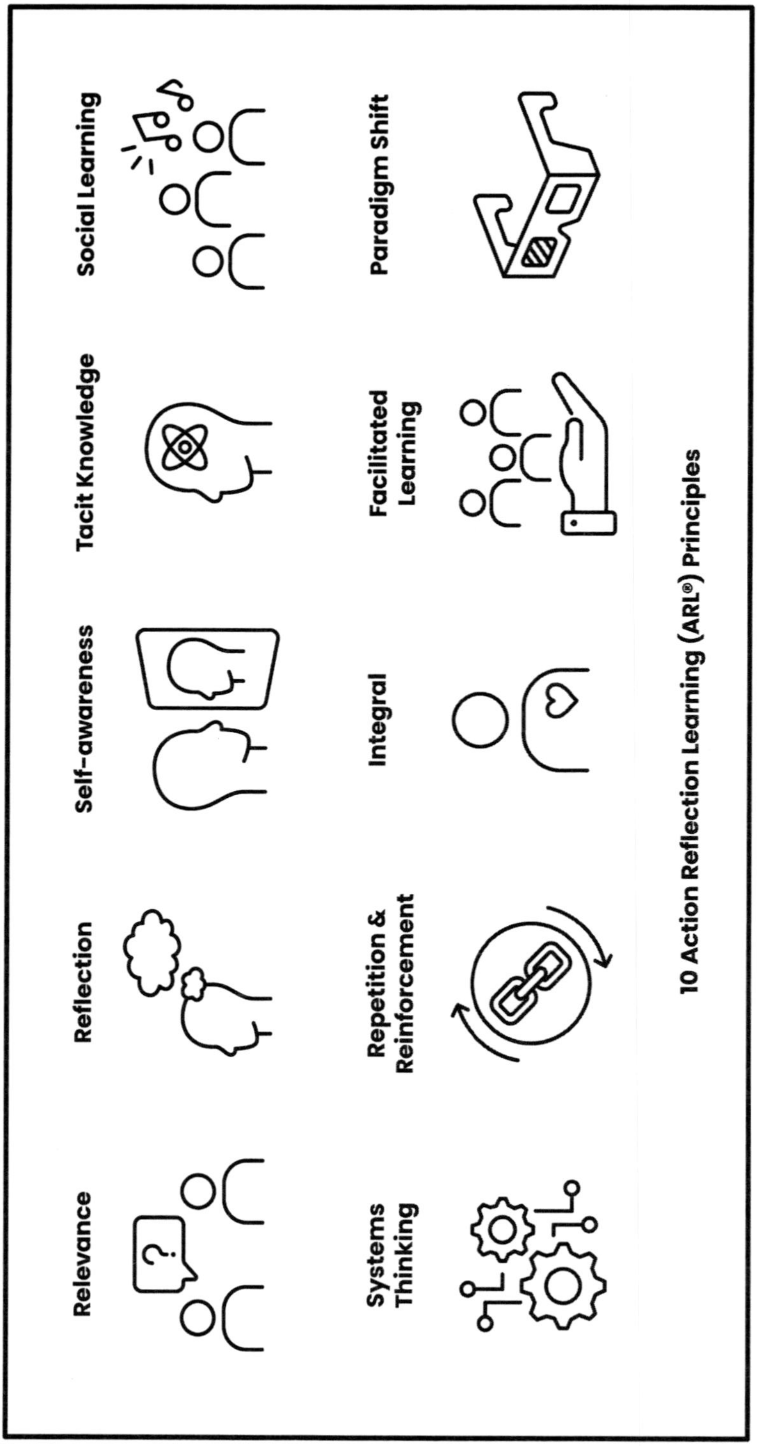

Figure 9-3: 10 Action Reflection Learning (ARL®) principles

Part 3

Opportunities For Application

CHAPTER 10
Implementing Effective Change

"How you change is how you succeed"

Nido Quebin
President of High Point University, North Carolina

The impact of Covid-19 on the entire globe is incalculable. Nations, organizations, and people everywhere had to confront the virus head-on, first to survive, and then to thrive in the face of the challenges and opportunities the pandemic has created. Covid-19 was a good example of how organizations, indeed society as a whole, must adapt to the new realities. As we have seen time after time in history, we know Covid-19 is not the last viral challenge. Scientists are already warning us to be ready for the next pandemic.

We also know that humans, resilient as we are, tend to be more comfortable with maintaining the *status quo*. Not surprisingly employees, like most people, tend to resist change. A 2021 Gartner survey of more than 800 HR leaders in 60 countries provided some interesting findings about possible causes for their reluctance. The main findings are:

1. Thirty-six percent (36%) of employees are fatigued from change

This is to be expected. The first twenty years of the 21st century have seen non-stop changes. Key events included the 2000 dotcom bust, 9/11 in 2001, 2003 SARS, the crippling 2008 global financial crisis and the rapid digital disruptions experienced by many sectors. The global onslaught of the Covid-19 pandemic caused huge changes that have been forced upon the global population, creating social, emotional, political and economic challenges and opportunities.

Organizations have been compelled to implement change as a response to each challenge or opportunity as it happened. Changes in strategies and plans necessitate re-structuring and re-organizing, often resulting in "casualties" whom the company must make redundant and let go. Employees who remained from the re-structuring exercise had to cope with the psychological stress and workload left behind by their departing colleagues. Just when everything started to settle down, another challenge strikes and we are back to making more changes.

It is no surprise that slightly more than one-third of employees are fatigued from constant change. The word "change" is not exciting or stimulating, and to many, it evokes negative emotions like fear of uncertainty, job losses and more work.

2. Thirty-seven percent (37%) of managers are not equipped to lead change

What causes employees to treat "change" negatively? Very telling in the Gardner 2021 report is the finding that almost 40% of managers are not equipped to lead the change itself. This is probably a major contributor to the negative experiences of employees. Most changes are uncomfortable and stressful in the first place. Employees have to go outside their comfort zones to cope with the change. Leaders who are well equipped will be in a better position to lead and support their teams to navigate the change terrain, reaching their destination in the best possible condition. Conversely, teams that are led by leaders who are not competent in driving change, are likely to encounter avoidable roadblocks and obstacles. These often caused unnecessary time and resources before they can reach their objectives.

3. Thirty-one percent (31%) of leaders and teams are not creating skill development solutions fast enough to meet changing skill needs

Leaders and teams are not learning fast enough to meet the fast-evolving skill needs. The report cites that teams are overwhelmed because their rate of skills development is not keeping pace with the rate of change. In most cases, the gaps are widening, and without the necessary skills, change becomes even more challenging. What is needed are new skills, attitudes and behaviors for both the immediate present and future. Leaders who are unable to implement changes successfully pay the price one way or another and this may include:

- Drop in performance due to the negative effects and disruptions caused by the ineffective change efforts
- Additional time, efforts and emotional energy needed to "repair" and "re-do" the badly planned or executed change initiative
- Demoralized team members, leading to employee disengagement and resignations
- Loss of confidence and trust in the leader and perhaps, also, the entire leadership team

Reasons for failure

According to McKinsey, 70% of change efforts did not achieve the change goals. Top reasons for the failure include:

1. The change is not led from the top

When senior management is not actively involved in, nor visibly supportive of the change, everyone down the line believes the change does not matter, given the management's lack of focus and attention. Without clear top management buy-in, it becomes difficult for any organizational-wide change to take place.

2. Failure to involve key stakeholders early in the process

The stakeholders can be both within and outside the organization. The latter group can include clients, partners, suppliers and government agencies. Without the input and ownership of these important people, the change plan is not complete. It is critical that stakeholders be involved as early as is possible. This will ensure their interests, views and concerns can be heard, addressed and taken into consideration during the planning process. It will be difficult to obtain their high buy-in and ownership of the change when you overlooked them. The right timing and timeliness of their involvement are key.

3. Unclear statement of purpose and lack of clarity in planning

This is related to the first point. It is essential that all levels of the organization understand and are aligned to the purpose of the effort and the expectations of senior management concerning the role to be played by every function and person.

4. Fear of change

Harry Levinson, the psychologist, and organizational consultant famously posited that "All change involves loss; and all loss must be mourned." Unless organizational leadership acknowledges, and makes plans to address this very human response, successful implementation of plans is jeopardized. The fear of change abounds in employees with questions such as: "Why is there a need to change?", "What if the change does not work?" and "What if I lose my job because of the change?". Unless addressed early, the lingering fear and anxiety will be a drag on the entire organization or team that is undergoing the change.

5. Significant attention is not paid to developing necessary skills and processes among change leaders

The change leader may not be trained to drive a change effort. Most of the time, the leader who is assigned with the task to manage a change initiative, is not properly equipped. The boss expected him "to know" or to learn by doing, going through the school of hard knocks. Such learning, without the proper skills and resources, comes with a price. This includes a failed change and damaged confidence and credibility of the change leader.

6. Good start, poor finish

Another reason for a change initiative to fail is the lack of a good finish. Some change efforts started on a high note but due to lack of follow-up and follow-through, the change was not sustained, and it drifted off-course. It is important for these change leaders to constantly assess if and how they are following the plans, what needs to be altered and what learnings need to be included in the revised plans.

Applying Shared Leadership Disciplines for successful change

Change will be more successfully implemented with Shared Leadership Disciplines®. Leaders who apply the 5 disciplines will naturally be inclusive, involving the right people, paying attention to their voices, collaborating and co-creating the change design, maintaining clear agreements and commitments and constantly challenging each other with good intent. Specifically, they approach the change process differently in the following ways:

1. **Involve their teams early**. They invite and bring the team members into the change discussion. This is done at the earliest moment when they are aware of the impending change and are ready to confide with them. The more time they give their people, the easier it is for the people to be open to and be receptive to the change.

2. **Hear all voices**. They make every effort to hear all the voices of their team, encouraging them to speak their hearts and minds. Too often, team members have little input in the change, and this is one reason for the general apathy among employees when it comes to taking ownership to implement the change at a later stage. Hearing all voices requires listening to the whole person (the Integral principle in Chapter 9). One good listening technique is to pay attention to the W.I.F.E. which is an acronym for:

- W - Words spoken by your people, and the meaning or intention behind the words
- I - Imagery or metaphor that is used. The visual or mental picture can be powerful
- F - Feelings and emotions of the people
- E - Energy level and body language, whether they are excited, upbeat or having negative emotions

3. **Act in partnership.** Another important approach that good leaders take is to invite their team members to co-design and co-create the change. They integrate as many as is possible the different views and ideas suggested by the team members. Doing so, leaders demonstrate their preparedness to be influenced by them. They see themselves as partners, not bosses of change.

4. **Make learning integral to the process.** How fast you change is how fast you will succeed. Effective change leaders understand that the change process, like most work processes, is dynamic and agility is needed to navigate the terrain. It requires the whole team, including the leaders themselves, to learn at the same time as they plan and implement the changes, adjusting and adapting all the time. As mentioned in the previous chapter, to succeed in change, the rate of ***Learning*** must be more or at least equal to the rate of ***Change***. Leadership In Motion's 10 Action Reflection Learning® principles and ARL tools help accelerate the learning at multi-dimensional levels.

RATE OF LEARNING ≥ RATE OF CHANGE

Figure 10-1: Learning greater than Change

To illustrate how the 5 Shared Leadership Disciplines® can guide a team's process, we take a case of a law firm that decided to operate virtually instead of operating from a physical office in Singapore. As a result of Covid-19, the firm's 17 team members have been operating from home and have demonstrated a capacity to function effectively via virtual video conferences. In light of the company's new objective to increase its global client base, the firm's leadership team decided to implement a strategy that will transform the firm from a brick-and-mortar enterprise to an almost 100% virtual outfit.

There are many countless companies thinking of implementing changes to seize the opportunities or overcome challenges that a crisis usually presents to the players. Using the above actual business situation as an example of effective shared leadership, the CEO Max (not his real name) implemented a transformational change by following these 5 disciplines:

1. The Discipline of "Connect"

Max would take specific steps that ensured the 17 team members would work well together. His first priority would be to ensure all the members of his diverse team are comfortable with each other, being open about their nationality, family, life-style, generational, tenure and experience differences. He would be creating a very open, conducive and collegial culture. The bond and trust built would help him to implement a smoother change.

Had the team being less connected, and the trust level not as high, Max would have to spend more time to help the 17 team members to relate and get to know each other more as persons. This is not a one-off activity. Continuing to "connect" will not only strengthen the inter-personal relationships, but also increase the care, concern and understanding among the team members.

Besides connecting at the personal level, Max would also spend time to connect the team with the purpose, mission, vision and core values of the company. While these are not new to the firm, going back to the basics and highlighting and refreshing the team on these fundamentals would help everyone to remember they are connected as one team, setting out to build a new future together.

2. The Discipline of "Collect"

The discipline of "Collect" is critical when managing change. A good place to start is to gather information from the team members as follows:

- Surfacing their hopes, fears and concerns about how the change will impact each of them and their functions
- Gathering their needs and feelings about how the change might affect them personally
- Collecting their questions on all aspects of the change process
- Collecting their opinions and ideas on what they believe will work, and what will not
- Understanding their learning aspirations and goals

A team with the openness to share and listen to each other without judgement, or the need to justify their questions or comments, can be liberating to the leader and the team members. This psychological safety is so vital for any team to excel in their games.

3. The Discipline of "Challenge"

Challenge is about encouraging the business, team and each member to think and act in new ways. This change may go against the desires of some of the people who may not see the need or the benefits of moving to a virtual organization. Max would have to inspire the team and find ways to change their minds and hearts, challenging them to go outside their comfort zone, and invite them to venture into a new way of working. He would also challenge the team to be bold, ambitious and have a high sense of urgency to digitize their operations and seize the opportunities created by the pandemic and the global digital transformation that is taking place at the same time.

The discipline of Challenge is also about Max giving permission to his team to challenge him or any of the leaders. This "I-am-opened-to-be-challenged-by-you" attitude adopted by Max is important as it elevates the influence and power of the team members to speak their minds and hearts.

Max knows that some in the team would still quietly resist the change, lack self-confidence or have unspoken ideas and suggestions. Max would encourage everyone to speak up openly, believing that every word that is spoken with good intention must be listened to. Max does not want a yes-team. Decisions that merely follow the leader or the majority's view are not always right for the organization or team. The discipline of Challenge is in support of Collaborate, even though at times, it may seem to be working in the opposite direction.

4. The Discipline of "Collaborate"

To collaborate is to work together to co-design and co-create the change plan. Letting the people who are affected by the change to explore the options and solutions is a powerful way to develop ownership and commitment. The key words are "involve" and "explore". Max would be ready to let his team members explore and offer suggestions to make the change work, and he would be prepared to discuss and decide on the trade-offs that will be necessary in the decision-making process.

Collaborate includes developing a shared vision and direction. Even though Max already has a bold vision of his legal firm serving the global market, he would choose to invite his team to co-create a vision that they care and are excited about. Max would be careful to make sure it is "our shared vision" and not "his vision". A powerful shared vision is like a magnet — it pulls everyone towards the vision, providing excitement and positive energy, thus increasing the probability of success as the firm transits from a physical set-up to a virtual office.

5. The Discipline of "Contract"

The discipline of Contract happens throughout the change process, right from the time of announcing the change, to discussing and exploring it, to making the decision and to implementing the change plan.

At the beginning of the process, Max would enable his team to agree on the norms by which they will discuss, explore and prepare for the change. Examples of norms could be 'respect for each other', 'speaking up' and 'taking 100% responsibility'. There could also be agreement for some of the members to assume certain roles and responsibilities. For example, having someone to be project manager, coordinator, meeting secretary and so on.

At each meeting, Max would ensure there is clear contracting with regards how each meeting is conducted, the agreement on follow-up actions, the timelines and deliverables. When the new structure and organization is clear, Max would contract with each of them on their roles, responsibilities and accountabilities. The discipline of Contract will ensure there would always be clear agreement, alignment and commitment throughout the change process. Whenever misalignment occurred, the team's norms would empower any team member to raise the issue and have it resolved.

Max made every effort to ensure all his team members apply the 5 disciplines throughout the change process — from the planning to the doing. As they practiced more and more in the sharing of the leadership, the 5 disciplines come to them more naturally, smoothly and the change journey has also become more enjoyable. Not only did they succeed in transforming to a virtual business, the team itself has also been transformed from within. The 5 disciplines have become their default operating mode to the way they operate as a professional, a team, an organization and business. Shared leadership had become their new culture.

Figure 10-2: Shared Leadership Disciplines®

So What? ...... Insights

Many leaders think of change in terms of them taking the role of "managing", "leading" or "driving" the change. These words connote a top-down or lead-from-the-front approach, which implies the leader is the one who assumes the driver's seat. Our point is that while the leader is accountable for the results of the work, he need not, indeed should not, attempt to assume all the responsibilities. What, in our experience is more effective and sustainable, is a sharing of leadership which relies on the following ingredients for successful change:

Many leaders think of change in terms of them taking the role of "managing", "leading" or "driving" the change. These words connote a top-down or lead-from-the-front approach, which implies the leader is the one who assumes the driver's seat.

1. Leadership and ownership are shared

The change leader has ultimate accountability, but he is not the only champion for the change. The leader and team members together own the change and take full responsibility for ensuring successful design and delivery of the change initiative.

2. Inclusivity and involvement bind the team

The leader involves the entire team in the whole change process from the earliest possible moment. This will ensure buy-in from the conceptualizing and formative stage of the change, enabling a good start, right from the onset of the change program.

3. All voices and all feelings are heard

The leader acknowledges that he values every person and encourages members to express and hear each other's thoughts and feelings. To do this, every member of the team must have the psychological safety and space to influence and shape the change, speaking up and stepping up at various times to ensure alignment and effective implementation of the change process.

4. Makes learning integral to the change process

The leader recognizes the importance and power of integrating and implementing Action Reflection Learning® principles and processes to the change process. Having the mindset and the discipline to do so will ensure the team's learning curve is in tandem, or better still, exceed the change cure. How fast and how well the team learns will be a key deciding factor, on how fast and well the envisaged change outcomes will be realized.

5. Put the 5 Shared Leadership Disciplines® constantly to work

The real power and benefits are when the leader puts all the 5 Shared Leadership Disciplines® to work. As in Max's situation, the 5 disciplines need not be followed in any rigorous order. Which discipline to apply will depend on the situation, needs and objectives at the point in time. What is important is to keep the 5 disciplines at the top of our mind and apply what is appropriate. This is the beauty of the 5 disciplines. With each application, you reinforce the sharing of leadership in the change process and can expect the following outcomes:

- Higher performance at the organizational and team dimensions
- Greater satisfaction at the professional and personal dimensions
- Greater returns on investment and profitability at the business dimension
- And ultimately contributing to the sustainability of the entity as well as creating a better planet.

CHAPTER 11

Leading Hybrid Teams

"The virus has broken through cultural and technological barriers .... setting in motion a structural shift where work takes place."

McKinsey Global Institute

Before the pandemic, the office was a must-have. Most of us have a fixed workspace, while others hot-desked, meaning you do not have a permanent work desk, but rather work on a desk that is available. The default mode is the office. In some cases, one must be physically visible in the office to prevent being "out of sight, out of mind".

Many hard-working employees have treated the office as their second home, spending 10 to 16 hours in the office and the remaining hours to commute, sleep and recharge before heading back to the office for another day's work. It is no wonder that organizations are willing to invest in the office environment to help employees stay happy, productive and literally be at "home".

With the pandemic, our close relationship with the office has been disrupted permanently. The "we must work in the office" mental model was jettisoned by many people. With extensive and repeated lockdowns to control the virus spread, the resilience and ingenuity of humans came into the fore. All of us hunkered in our homes and successfully proved that working from home is an equally good option.

With the extended experience of working from home, new norms and habits have been formed. Many of us got used to working outside the office. We saved time commuting to work on congested roads. We were able to spend more time with our family members. Some of us moved out of the city to the suburbs for cheaper rent and a better quality of life.

A research study reported in Harvard Business Review in August 2020 that people who worked from home were able to focus on tasks that really matter. The number of tasks rated as "tiresome" dropped by half, from 27% to 12% and people did 50% more work activities through their personal choice.

According to research by the Boston Consulting Group and The Network, 89% of workers expected to work from home at least some of the time after the Covid-19 crisis. This finding emerged from a survey of almost 209,000 people in 190 countries. This clearly shows that 9 out of 10 persons do not want to go back to the pre-Covid days. They want to be able to spend a portion of each week working from home. In other words, hybrid work is the new normal in many organizations.

Why does this matter to leaders?

There were periods in history which transformed work and society. The industrial revolution brought people from the farms to the factories. The invention of the internet created an inter-connected globalized world and people found themselves working harder and longer hours, either in the office or busy shuttling between countries and cities. Covid-19 will be seen in history as a once-in-a-lifetime transformation. This time it brings the home and family back to the center of people's lives, thus changing the where, when and how we work in very fundamental ways. There is no going back to the pre-pandemic way of working as the "experiment" of working from home has, ironically, been hugely successful. As a result, many organizations are adopting the hybrid work arrangement. For example, it could be three days in the office and two days working from home. The implications for leaders are:

1. Leadership styles have to be adjusted

- Leadership styles that work well for in-person management must be adjusted for hybrid teams. When the team is in the office, there are opportunities for quick meetings, dropping in at each other's desk to discuss work progress, engaging in social chats and subconsciously managing by sight — taking comfort seeing everyone is seemingly busy at work. When not all the team members are present in the workplace at the same time, some leaders can become uncomfortable and even anxious.

2. Team norms for hybrid operations must be aligned

- Norms are expectations of attitudes and behaviors. New team norms are needed when members are not seeing each other regularly. Failure to define and agree to new norms causes unnecessary frictions and stress. One common complaint is people feel their work and personal lives are now blurred when working from home. They feel they are working longer hours at home with little personal space. The leader is often seen as contributing to an unsettled environment. One senior manager in a Singapore-based organization organized virtual discussions with his team members at night, often starting at 9 or 10 pm. His reason: His workday was taken up by endless internal and external meetings and it was only at night that he could find the time to discuss work issues faced by his team. His failure to manage his time and to jointly establish clear norms resulted in stress and frustration among his team members.

3. New skills & tools are needed

- The skills that work well when managing in person may not work well when operating with hybrid teams. Take for example communication skills. When speaking with someone in person, we can see and sense the whole person, including their body language, emotions and energy. When communicating virtually, we normally can only see the facial expressions. Astonishingly, some leaders conduct virtual meetings without requiring cameras to be turned on. Not only does this make it even more difficult to "read" and engage the people in the room, but it often guarantees that participants used the meeting to multi-task and engage in other activities. It is critical that leaders apply new skills and tools to navigate successfully and enjoyably in this new landscape.

Challenges of leading hybrid teams

Leading hybrid teams brings the following challenges for leaders and their teams:

1. The challenge of trust and confidence

In a research study published by the Harvard Business Review in 2020, 38% of the managers interviewed were not confident that their team members were able to perform remotely as compared to working physically at the workplace. Lack of trust by the leader was determined to be the central issue.

Without trust and confidence in the team members, leaders usually focus their efforts on micro-managing the process, directing every step so that the work gets done according to their expectations. Such an approach only encourages members to be "compliant followers" and reinforce the trust-deficit environment, giving rise to demotivation and disengagement.

Alan worked in Shanghai as the Regional Human Resource Director and reported to the Chief Human Resource Officer based in London. Most of the time, his London boss wrote long emails detailing the steps and actions that he wanted Alan to do. Initially Alan tried to give his comments and ideas. Very soon Alan learned not to waste time and energy, being aware that the boss was a micro-manager who was certain that he alone knew how to deliver the goods. The end result: Alan learned to wait for instructions from his boss, instead of taking the initiative to speak up, step up and do even more in his job role. Alan's boss had dampened Alan's passion, creativity, ownership and commitment. The subtle message was that he did not trust Alan's ability.

Imagine this scenario multiplied daily across organizations. Micro-managers soon become fire fighters simply because they don't have the bandwidth to tell all the Alans in their company what to do. Low sense of ownership leads to higher disengagement and lower morale. Ultimately productivity and profitability suffer. We have witnessed this failure across many organizations and businesses.

2. The challenge of engaging team members to speak up, step up and take more ownership

"My team members are quiet during our virtual meetings. How can I get them to speak up more and be more proactive?"

This is a common challenge faced by leaders who are so used to in-person communication. Jim is a marketing communications manager in a state government department in Malaysia. He has a team of 14 members who are physically working in the local residential precincts in Johore Bahru. Before Covid-19, whenever he called a meeting, all his 14 team members would travel to his HQ office for an in-person meeting.

Covid-19 has completely changed the way he holds his meetings. With virtual meetings, he immediately experienced the following challenges:

- Only a handful were participating in the discussion. In each meeting, he found himself doing most of the talking as there were very little interaction.
- When discussing specific issues, he was not able to get his team members to engage and discuss the issues. His team members were habitually waiting for his instructions.
- To make it worse, in his organization, the unspoken norm for virtual meetings was to keep the camera turned OFF. Effectively he was left with a black-out monitor screen, and often, he felt like he was talking to a blank wall.

What could Jim do? What would you do if you were in Jim's situation?

3. The challenge of managing bosses and upper management

When your bosses, including upper management, are in the same office as you, you have opportunities to meet and engage them. These include exchanging small talks or providing quick updates in their office, along the corridor or even in the washroom! When there are issues, you can easily meet in their office to address how to progress.

Once you, your colleagues and your bosses operate remotely, these opportunities disappear. Your main tools are emails, messaging apps, telephone and video meetings.

Bob, a Bangkok-based department head responsible for multimedia entertainment projects, was frustrated with his senior management team who were based in various cities in Europe and Asia. He had alerted the senior management team that one of the projects would not meet the delivery timeline due to the lack of manpower. At one virtual management meeting where Bob was providing a quarterly project update, instead of showing empathy and seeking to understand the situation better, the Regional CEO expressed his disappointment with Bob. Bob was placed on the defensive and felt he lost face and credibility in front of the entire senior management team. Upon his self-reflection, Bob knew that he had not managed his bosses well. This is the challenge of working remotely. If you were Bob, how can you better manage your upper management?

4. The challenge of too many meetings and working longer hours

This is one of the major pet peeves that employees have when working from home. When in the office, people will come to you to discuss, ask for help or get things from you. You are used to it and perhaps even enjoy the socializing part as well. The bantering, jokes and gossips are all part of the day's work. When you leave the office, no matter what time it is, you can choose to be done with work. The next day, you will go through the routine again. Even though you are working more hours, there is a clear line between work and off-work.

When working from home, you will be invited to endless meetings. People that cannot visit you for that discussion will set up a meeting with you. We zoomed so much that we become "zoombies". The shared calendar, with all its benefits, has its major setback -- you no longer have control over your time. "While remote work affords employees greater flexibility, it also makes disconnecting extremely difficult," said Paul McDonald, senior executive director of Robert Half. "Many people feel pressure to keep up with rising workloads and are putting in long hours to support the business and customer needs. But everyone needs time to rest and recharge to give their best".

Einstein once said: "We cannot solve our problems with the same thinking we used when we created them". The challenges of managing hybrid and remote teams as described above cannot be solved using our current mental models. We will continue to produce the same food with the same taste if we keep using the same recipe. There is a better recipe to leading and coaching hybrid teams.

How do Shared Leadership Disciplines® make a difference to leading hybrid teams

In essence, the 5 Shared Leadership Disciplines® create the team environment and expectations that allow every member in the team to:

Figure 11-1: Shared Leadership Disciplines®

1. Be valued and respected

- The discipline of ***"Connect"*** ensures that every member is inter-personally connected with each other. At the beginning of each meeting, time is allocated to engage in short and enriching chats to touch base with each other, getting to know and understand each other better as fellow human beings, rather than merely as colleagues or associates.

2. Be safe & be yourself

- Most people perform best when they are authentic and connected with themselves and others. The discipline of ***"Connect"*** creates the informality and psychological safety that allows the disciplines of ***"Contract", "Collect", "Collaborate"*** and ***"Challenge"*** to flourish.

3. Be aligned and accountable

- The discipline of ***"Contract"*** ensures all members are properly aligned to what, why and how the work, projects and tasks will be done. Regardless of how many days are spent in the office or home, when there is proper alignment, gaining the agreement and commitment of members and ensuring accountability will be easier.

4. Be inclusive and complete

- The 5 disciplines ensure that each member in the team is remembered, included and involved. In hybrid teams, it is easy to miss out the persons who are not physically present at the workplace. Ensuring you reach out to hear each and every voice is critical as this demonstrates how much you value your team members. Their participation will naturally lead to a higher vested interest and buy-in of the tasks and goals required of them.

5. Be co-creators, co-owners and collaborators

- The disciplines of ***"Collaboration"*** and ***"Challenge"*** break down the silos between individuals within and outside the team. The collaborative mindset brings the different members together, both from within and outside the team. Members have the psychological safety and freedom to challenge current ways of doing things, finding new and innovative solutions and providing mutual support and encouragement to each other. The co-creation process enables all members to have a higher sense of purpose, ownership and engagement, leading to the team working more cohesively together to achieve even higher performance and outcomes.

Some of the tools and ideas that you can use to bring each of the Shared Leadership Disciplines to come alive are highlighted in Chapters 4 to 8. You can also refer to the summary found at the end of this book.

So What? ...... Insights

Leading a team in-person already poses difficulties for many leaders. Just as leaders are grappling with this question and learning the ropes of becoming inspiring leaders, they are thrown into another end of the pool. A common question among leaders is: "How can we inspire, motivate and coach our teams to higher performance when we do not see them regularly?"

What is needed is to first accept that we are in a new normal and recognize that we cannot use old approaches for new situations. There must be a better way to lead and coach our teams.

What is needed is to first accept that we are in a new normal and recognize that we cannot use old approaches for new situations. There must be a better way to lead and coach our teams. Sharing leadership does not occur by simply stating that we will. It must be learned and practiced. The 5 Shared Leadership Disciplines® is the recipe to help any leader make his hybrid team engaged, productive and having fun.

As team leaders and team coaches we have an exciting opportunity to invite our hybrid teams to join us in creating a new way of working together. Just ask your team for help. Let them share in the leadership of your team.

CHAPTER 12

Solving VUCA Problems

"You can't solve today's problems with yesterday's solutions"

Albert Einstein
German-American Physicist

The role of a leader is to lead and influence a group of people to achieve common goals. To do this well, the leader engages in a never-ending process of planning, organizing, leading, communicating and motivating his or her people to ensure there is sufficient clarity, commitment and energy to complete the work. In the process of achieving their goals, the leader and the team solve numerous problems, major and minor, anticipated and unexpected.

The ability to solve problems and make effective decisions is integral to the leader's, and to the team members' job roles. In our world that is increasingly more volatile, uncertain, complex and ambiguous (VUCA), the need to be able to solve problems effectively has been identified in the Future of Jobs Survey 2020 report published by the World Economic Forum as among the top 15 skills for 2025. Interestingly, problem solving is cited twice in the list of 15 skills (see Table 12-1, items 3 and 10). This underscores the importance of this competency.

1	Analytical thinking and innovation	9	Resilience, stress tolerance and flexibility
2	Active learning and learning strategies	10	Reasoning, problem-solving and ideation
3	Complex problem-solving	11	Emotional intelligence
4	Critical thinking and analysis	12	Troubleshooting and user experience
5	Creativity, originality and initiative	13	Service orientation
6	Leadership and social influence	14	Systems analysis and evaluation
7	Technology use, monitoring and control	15	Persuasion and negotiation
8	Technology design and programming		

Source: Future of Jobs Survey 2020, World Economic Forum

Table 12-1: Top 15 skills for 2025

This chapter looks at how VUCA problems can be better solved using the shared leadership approach.

The Complex World

David Snowden, a Welsh management consultant, classifies problems into 4 categories:

1. Simple
2. Complicated
3. Complex
4. Chaotic

Simple problems are routine problems that can be solved using best practices or procedures. For complicated problems, one knows the questions to ask but does not have the expertise to address them. The solution is to engage others with the expertise. For example, if you want to automate your operational processes, you need to hire consultants with the requisite know-how.

For complex problems, there are "unknown unknowns". You do not know the questions to ask. A good example is the wave after wave of infections during the Covid-19 pandemic. As the virus took its toll on countries around the world, governments "experimented" with various actions to contain the virus. The actions were adjusted as they gained more knowledge and experience, including learning from the experiences of other countries.

For chaotic situations, things are crazy and out-of-control. The initial priority is to contain the problem and then look for real solutions. The initial Covid-19 outbreak is a good example. Governments reacted by quickly closing borders and locking down cities and towns to contain the spread while frantically looking for more scientifically-based answers to the many unknowns and uncertainty.

Most of the time, leaders are solving complicated and complex problems. Knowing the type of problem that we are solving is important. Some organizations are quick to engage external consultants to the chagrin of their internal staff. Ivan, a senior department leader in a global company, was flabbergasted that his company paid more than US$1 million to a top global consulting firm to solve a certain complex issue that they had. What the consultants did was to engage the employees for their views and ideas before compiling and presenting the information in a glossy fashion, adding some of their own insights and recommendations. Does this sound familiar? Consultants are good at asking questions, drawing out the inputs and making meaning of the collected information for the client. Ivan rightly felt the company could have done the same study with their internal resources. This would have achieved far better outcomes at a fraction of US$1 million.

The reality is we do not have endless financial resources to engage external consultants. Furthermore, while external consultants can provide expertise for "complicated" problems, they may not be better than us and our team in solving "complex" and "chaotic" situations. Our own people understand the operating environment and context better than external people. The money for the consultants' professional fees is better spent on incentivizing staff to solve the problem and see to the successful implementation of the solution.

One common mistake by leaders is not thinking holistically or systematically about outcomes that will meet the expectations of all their key stakeholders.

Too often, leaders are encouraged to think and look primarily 'outside' of the box for innovative solutions. We have come to realize that many times, effective solutions can lie 'inside' the box as well. Employees doing the actual work often have ideas and solutions, only if we tap into them using the right approach and tools.

The Pentagon-Plus System Approach

In solving problems, be it of a routine, complicated, complex, or chaotic nature, we look for effective solutions that achieve the desired outcomes, not from a narrow angle, but from multiple angles. The question is: What angles do we need to consider? Many leaders run into problems even when they believe they have found a solution, because they find that the solution does not meet the expectation of certain stakeholders.

One common mistake by leaders is not thinking holistically or systematically about outcomes that will meet the expectations of all their key stakeholders. Leaders often react immediately to focus on solving the burning issue and ignore assessing it from higher, wider and deeper angles. The pressure to solve the challenge prevents them from taking the time to stop and reflect. And this failure can be compounded when the leader has no systemic model to assist him in thinking through the challenge holistically and strategically.

A useful framework to help us in the thinking process is the Pentagon-Plus System Model. Leaders use this tool to think of impact, outcomes and implications on six dimensions, thus bringing a broader and more holistic approach to the challenges. First mentioned in Chapter 5 for contracting, the six dimensions presented here pertain to problem solving and reinforces the importance of the Pentagon-Plus in leadership and team coaching.

Figure 12-1: Pentagon-Plus System Model

1. The Business dimension

This dimension focuses primarily on the clarity of the business mission (what the organization is here to do), the purpose (why it does what it does), the vision (a picture of the desired future), its customers and partners (whom it does business with) and the business model and strategy (how it earns its revenue and/or how it delivers its services and value). Key stakeholders include the shareholders (owners), board members, external customers, partners, employees, suppliers and sometimes NGOs and government agencies. This dimension encourages leaders to identify their business challenges and specify the business outcomes needed.

2. The Organizational dimension

This dimension focuses on the organization's internal structure and organization to implement and achieve its mission, vision, purpose and goals. The key drivers of success include establishing the organization's optimal leadership, culture, values, systems, policies, people and rewards systems. Its success can be measured in terms of effectiveness, efficiency, productivity, quality, talent retention, employee feedback and financial returns. One important outcome is the effective alignment of differences that can exist between the many functions, departments and teams within the organization.

3. The Team dimension

Every team should have its purpose, mission, norms, processes, goals and targets. All these will naturally be reflective of the broader organizational direction. This dimension focuses on how the team wants to work together, how it is actually succeeding in doing this, how it is applying the shared leadership disciplines, the team culture and norms, and what team skills must be developed in order to move up its performance curve.

4. The Professional dimension

This dimension pertains to the professional aspects of the individual team members, including having the right competencies, professional development plans, motivation, learning and growth.

5. The Personal dimension

The personal dimension focuses on the individual member as a unique human being. Team members come with personal hopes, dreams, likes and dislikes, needs and wants for themselves, their families, friends and the community.

6. The Sustainability dimension

The sustainability dimension in this context has a twofold meaning:

a. The planet's sustainability, based on specific outcomes for protecting our planet, our environment and the people on our planet for current and future generations. Decisions made by any organization can create environmental and social problems or possibilities.
b. The sustainability of the organization from the economic (business), organizational, team, professional and/or personal perspectives.

Viewing problems and solving them using a multi-dimensional approach such as the Pentagon-Plus Model is important because it is a recognition that we are operating within a larger system with high inter-connectivity and inter-dependency among the parts. A solution may work well according to one dimension but might have a negative impact when on other dimensions. By using the Pentagon-Plus, we maximize our problem solving and decision-making abilities as we are encouraged to view challenges and opportunities more systemically.

- For example, a solution requiring employees to work longer hours on a prolonged basis may be good as a short-term solution to solve a team's manpower shortages, but it is not sustainable when viewed from the Organizational, Professional, Personal and ultimately the Business dimensions. The longer hours take a toll on employees' personal lives and they no longer enjoy their work. This might lead to people leaving the company, which could itself have a domino effect with more resignations. The holistic perspective must prevail to take all dimensions into account to fulfill the mission.

- A company may have thought it had solved its production waste problem by dumping its chemical waste illegally in a small obscure river. Not only did the chemicals harm the river and its ecosystems, but it also released toxic fumes. This was a real situation in a town in a Southeast Asian country that affected 6,000 people, with 2,775 requiring hospitalization. And instances like this have and are still occurring all around the world. All of us are affected directly or indirectly. We are the world.

We will explore this critical area of Sustainability in Chapter 15, including how leaders should think and act when solving problems to reach their goals.

Why a Shared Leadership team is better equipped to solve complex problems

What advantages does a shared leadership team have over teams using a top-down leadership model when operating in a highly VUCA environment?

1. Higher team trust

Complex and chaotic situations call for innovative solutions and actions. Without a foundation of high level of trust among the leaders and members, teams can be embroiled in endless debates, with members reluctant to share their real thoughts and feelings. Leaders are hampered in responding quickly to develop effective plans amid the uncertainty of the complex and chaotic situations. Even when the leaders have designed good plans, lack of trust and alignment serve as stumbling blocks to successful implementation. Trust is not built overnight, and it cannot be obtained at will.

Teams practicing the 5 disciplines of ***connect, contract, collect, collaborate and challenge*** on a daily basis will, over time, deepen team trust. This will enable more open communications, higher commitment, a willingness to speak up and increased comfort in trying out new problem-solving approaches.

2. Collective wisdom

Complex and chaotic situations lead to uncertainty, which in turn surfaces unclear and incomplete information. Further, an unsettled atmosphere can produce an overhanging fear that it may worsen unless urgent actions are taken.

Under such circumstances, the ability to speedily tap into the collective wisdom of the team is critical. A leader who has habitually practiced the discipline of "*collect*" has demonstrated to the team a proven process to hear all voices and gather inputs at short notice. Moreover, this collective wisdom is not confined to the team only. As with concentric circles, "collect" can be extended from the center which is your team, to the various stakeholders on the outside. The book of Proverbs says: "Where there is no counsel, plans fail. But in a multitude of counselors, they are established".

Teams practicing the 5 disciplines of connect, contract, collect, collaborate and challenge on a daily basis will, over time, deepen team trust.

3. Courage to try new things

Complex situations call for new thinking. You cannot fall back on the past for your answers if there are no relevant precedents to guide you. It is worth noting that of the 15 World Economic Forum's desirable future skills (Table 12-1), 2 important skills address the challenges of trying new things: No. 5 on "creativity, originality and initiative" and No. 9 on "resilience, stress tolerance and flexibility". Both skills require significant courage to admit what you know and do not know, and to invite your team members to co-create new solutions and to venture into new arenas. During the process, leaders welcome and invite all voices, including opposing views and ideas. When the leader demonstrates his "openness to be challenged", it creates another layer of psychological safety for the team members. The resultant action plan, new and untried as it is, will have the backing and commitment from every team member.

4. Clear alignment on responsibility and accountability

Sharing leadership is about enabling every member to take on more ownership and leadership. It establishes clear responsibilities for every team member – what is to be done, by whom and by when. Teams that regularly practice the discipline of "contract" will have higher confidence in the commitment to act and follow-through on what has been agreed. While the team takes on more responsibility and leadership, the leader will continue to take final accountability for the team's results.

5. Speed in response and implementation

Speed of response is critical when dealing with complex and chaotic problems. Delayed actions can cause serious damage and even lives, as was evident during the Covid-19 pandemic. Speed is critical to collecting relevant information such as facts, thoughts, feelings, past experiences and ideas before you decide your next step of co-designing a solution and gaining the commitment from key stakeholders to act. How fast you can access your team's collective tacit knowledge and wisdom can make a difference to the outcomes. A team that is well-grooved and honed in the 5 Shared Leadership Disciplines® has created effective channels of open communications that permit energy to be galvanized quickly. Response will be quicker to get all hands on deck, as compared to a team that is still operating in the traditional pyramid mindset.

6. Fail fast and learn fast

In dealing with complexities and chaos, there will be mistakes and failures as the team experiments with various ideas. The mindset and readiness to "fail fast and learn fast" is critical to the success of any team operating in the VUCA environment. The ability to learn from one's own and others' experiences is key. It is significant that the World Economic Forum placed "active learning and learning strategies" as the second most important and desirable future skills (Table 12-1).

The foundation of the Shared Leadership Disciplines® framework is undergirded by the 10 Action Reflection Learning® principles which we have explained in Chapter 9. The significance of these 10 principles is that they enable the team's rate of learning to be equal to, or greater than the rate of change. In other words, a shared leadership team will be able to stay on top of the game, as failing fast and learning fast becomes part of its success playbook and culture.

So What? ...... Insights

There are many ways of viewing and solving VUCA problems. Building on the Action Reflection Learning® principle of Systems Thinking, problems should be viewed holistically and systematically. One powerful framework is the Pentagon-Plus System Model. This model examines problems from the business, organizational, team, professional, personal and sustainability dimensions.

Understanding the different types of problems also helps us to adopt the appropriate approach. In today's fast changing world, leaders are faced with more and more complicated, complex, and chaotic situations. The leader and team who embrace and use the Shared Leadership Disciplines® regularly and consistently will have built-in advantages in terms of:

- Having a foundation of higher team trust
- Quick access to collective wisdom
- Courage to speak up, create and implement
- Higher speed in problem solving and decision making
- Faster rate of learning and responding to the dynamic situation

Such a team will far outperform the traditional model that is driven by the leader at the top of the pyramid.

CHAPTER 13

Developing Our People

"The growth and development of people is the highest calling of leadership"

Harvey Firestone
Founder, Firestone Tire and Rubber Company

As practical leaders, we know we cannot do all the things ourselves. We can have the best strategy and plans, but almost always, our achievements are dependent on the people that we need to work with. This is the reason why organizations and leaders pay attention and invest time and resources to develop their people.

One of our coaches was coaching Sharon, a Finance Director in a technology company based in the Philippines. Sharon told our coach that she only has one coaching goal for the 3-month coaching program: "To be a leader who develops new leaders". Our coach was impressed with the way she views her leadership position and how she intends to add value to the team and the company. It brings to mind the thought-provoking words of Mary Parker Follett whom we first mentioned in Chapter 3 — "the most essential work of the leader is to create more leaders".

Sharon's mindset came from her immediate supervisor, James who was a senior Finance Director in the company. She started in the company as a finance manager and over the past 5 years, had been promoted twice — first to a senior manager, and now her current director position. James had since been re-assigned to another part of the business. Of all the immediate supervisors that she had in her past 16 years of work, Sharon felt James was the boss who had made the biggest impact on her professional growth and success. She remembered him to be someone who cared for her professional development as much as he cared for her work results. Sharon was grateful that she was blessed with such a leader. She still held him with the highest regard.

The reality is that most leaders are too overly focused on work performance. People development are not their highest priority. Yet, these leaders are the first to declare that their people are their biggest asset.

There are leaders who are similar to James. They care for the development of their team members at the same time as holding them accountable to their work results. However, the reality is that most leaders are too overly focused on work performance. People development are not their highest priority. Yet, these leaders are the first to declare that their people are their biggest asset.

The People Factor

In economic terms, there are three important factors in the production of goods and services:

1. Land - the physical space and natural resources
2. Capital - the assets, capital goods and financial resources

3. People - the talents, ideas, and the indomitable human spirit

Of these factors, people easily top the list. "People" include the entrepreneurs and innovators who combine ideas, land and capital to add value and serve society better. It is the people who will make the world a more sustainable place to live in. In today's world, "land" and "capital" are relatively easy to obtain. You can attract capital with innovative ideas and choose where to produce your goods and services.

Attracting and gathering talented people is a complex process. It involves finding, attracting, recruiting, motivating and then developing them. These deliberate steps are necessary as salary and benefit costs usually form a major proportion of the team's cost structure. Having obtained approval for the additional headcount, your next task is to hire the right person. There are three inter-related challenges to manage:

- **Right Fit** — Bearing in mind the budget, you have to find the people with the right skill sets and who fit well into your organization's culture. In short - the right skills, right fit and right price. In some cases, when your team is scaling up quickly, the right number as you may need to hire several applicants with these requirements at the same time.

- **Right Location** — Despite the changing attitudes towards employees working remotely, organizations need people to be in a specific physical location -- the right country and city. Even though we are operating virtually more than before, people are still needed on the ground to know the actual terrain, build the relationships and drive the actions. You may have found the right person, but when this person is in a distant city or country, mobility and expatriate costs become factors that complicate your hiring decision.

- **Right Time** — You need the people to be available at the right time, when you need them. For new projects, timing is important since if you hire too far in advance of the project start, you might have to pay salaries from Day One. Hiring too late can mean delays and lost opportunity.

It can be difficult to have these three aspects come together in a timely fashion especially when hiring outside talent. Therefore, it makes commercial and common sense to invest and develop current employees to fill these positions internally, and only when necessary, to hire from the outside. This can be achieved with a disciplined process that includes partnering closely with the key people and co-designing customized development plans for each talent and ensuring a high level of ownership for successful implementation.

The concept of grooming one's own talents and successors is easier said than done. Despite the many years of investing in talent and leadership development, most organizations are facing the same human resource challenges today as they had in the past. The 2021 Gartner survey of 800 HR leaders revealed dissatisfaction with the efforts to date:

- 35% of HR leaders surveyed believed the succession management processes do not yield the right leaders at the right time.
- 27% of these same HR leaders believed their organizations are struggling to develop mid-level leaders.

Why organizations find people development challenging

The need to develop people is indisputable. However, it comes with challenges such as these that we often hear:

1. "I don't have enough time to spend on developing my people"

This is by far the most common challenge. You and your people are facing time pressure every day. Few people can escape from the need to deal with the high workload and the pressure to deliver. Leaders are busy juggling their limited time to meet the expectations of their bosses and customers. It is no surprise that while they view the development of their people as important, it is not high in their priority. They believe the next best thing that they can do is to outsource staff development to HR and to external coaches and trainers. Or to kick the can down the road until they have "more time".

The solution need not be an "either / or". We can have both. Leaders perhaps should be learning an approach that while the team is addressing the business challenges, the same team members are also learning and developing their skills at the same time.

2. "Developing my team members does not guarantee their loyalty"

You may have experienced the frustration of losing your people after you had taken much time, effort and heart to groom them. You question where their loyalty is. The short answer is – the focus of loyalty has changed. Among the Boomer generation, loyalty to the employer used to be as solid as an oak tree. But in the 1990s when organizations relocated, re-structured and downsized due to business and economic reasons, many employees ended up with the short end of the employment stick.

Employees started to focus their loyalty on themselves and their families. They look for the best overall returns for themselves, professionally and personally. Generation Y and Z employees tend to focus on jobs they consider meaningful and that give them a strong sense of purpose. Perhaps they have been encouraged by their crisis-hardened parents and seniors to do what is best for their own career and life. YOLO – You Only Live Once. Going by this dictum, they are not worried about leaving their jobs when the time is right, when they feel they do not have the right boss or when they do not find a strong purpose or meaning in their job.

Many leaders have this lingering question in their minds: "But what if I develop my employees and they don't stay?" While it is a valid concern, an even more important question to ask is: "What if you don't develop them and they stay?"

3. "My organization is flat. There are fewer opportunities for advancement"

In today's flatter structures, there are fewer positions that employees can grow into. This is not a new phenomenon. In past team structures, it was common to have "deputy" or "second-in-charge" positions. These provided excellent learning and growth opportunities for succession planning and grooming. With constant delayering and cost-cutting, teams and organizations are leaner, with multi-hatting and matrix reporting becoming the norm. What is surprising is not the situation itself, but the fact that after more than 30 years of operating with these same challenges, many leaders and organizations are still searching for effective ways to address the succession issue.

Leaders should ask themselves: "What is missing?". "What will it take to better prepare the potential successors in the teams?"

4. "My organization does not have sufficient resources to develop my people"

Many leaders believe that their organization has neither the financial means nor the people to conduct their internal development programs. It is a big obstacle to the leaders as they are also faced with other work priorities. After putting up initial fights for more resources, most leaders regrettably learn to live with the "no budget" situation. They chose to focus on delivering their team or business results at the expense of their people's learning and growth.

What key steps can leaders take to address these challenges?

Here's what you can do to achieve professional development of your team members while developing your business and your organization at the same time.

First, embrace a shared leadership coaching mindset

1. "I will take responsibility for the learning and growth of my people"

Regardless of financial resources, we cannot leave the responsibility of staff development to others. We must take ownership. We know our team members well. We can coach our people while at work with them. We can use effective team coaching techniques whenever the learning opportunity presents itself. We can change the way we lead, seeking and offering feedback, creating an environment where our team members find it easy to speak up, step up and to try new things. Our taking ownership to grow our people will be felt by everyone in and outside the team. It will be hard for our people not to be positively influenced by our drive and heart to develop them.

2. "I will use every working experience for learning"

Working and learning are two activities that can and should go together. Unfortunately, many leaders only think in binary terms. They still live by the mental model that working and learning are separate and mutually exclusive. This self-limiting compartmentalized thinking needs to change.

One of LIM's core beliefs is that we can learn and earn at the same time. In fact, we hold that the workplace is the perfect arena for personal and professional development. Attending business school courses that base their teaching on simulated business cases is time-consuming and expensive. That is why our leadership development programs are based on each organization's actual and current challenges, and participants learn new skills and behaviors while solving their real challenges. We call it "Earning while Learning". Taking the time to reflect during the work itself leads to powerful learning insights. As highlighted in Chapter 9, John Dewey, American philosopher and educator, posited that people do not simply learn from their experiences. They learn by reflecting on their experiences. In other words, we can integrate intentional learning with our team's work activities.

Second, anticipate and identify the future needs

3. Anticipate the strategic-future and establish the developmental needs ahead

A practical starting point to develop your people is to identify and improve their current competency gaps. This can be a combination of knowledge, skills, behaviors and experiences that are necessary for the performance of their present job. Address these competency gaps and produce noticeable changes in their performance in the immediate or short term.

As a leader, you also need to lift their eyes and look beyond the horizon and focus on the competencies that are needed in the next 2 to 3 years and beyond. This will enable you to prepare your team strategically for the future. Addressing opportunities and acquiring the competencies required of these opportunities is considered one of the hallmarks of responsible, caring and forward-looking leaders.

Every leader is an HR leader. You have to be directly involved in growing your people.

As leaders we need to be bi-focal on the current and future competency gaps and opportunities. As Figure 13-1 shows, leadership is about keeping both priorities constantly in the line of sight and achieving them.

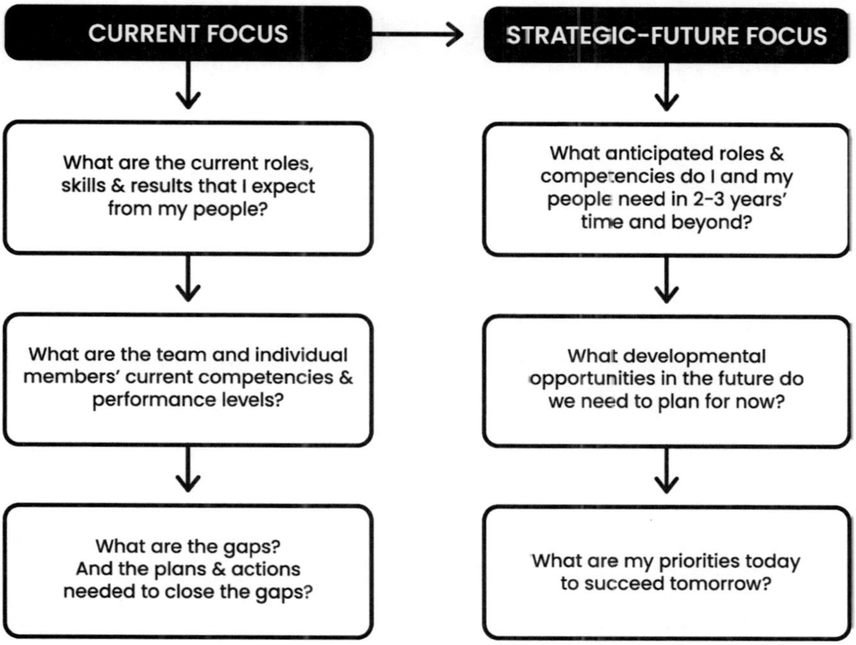

Figure 13-1: Current and Strategic Focus

Third, co-create talent development plans with shared ownership

4. Increase ownership using the 5 Shared Leadership Disciplines®

Every leader is an HR leader. You have to be directly involved in growing your people. The 5 Shared Leadership Disciplines® provide the framework to help you co-design and co-create a talent development plan with increased level of shared ownership and accountability from the boss, HR and your people.

a. Discipline of Collect

Begin by *collecting* information from your key stakeholders to learn what they hope to see and get from your talent development plans. Collecting also includes lessons from the past, learning what has worked or not worked well.

- Your boss: Your boss must support you as you take the initiative to create concrete plans to develop your people, including your potential successor(s). By getting his inputs at this early stage, you are also involving your boss as a close partner. Align with him and detail the specific support you want from him.

- HR (including Talent Development leaders): HR will certainly be delighted to have you step up and take responsibility for your people's growth. You can listen to HR's hopes, expectations and where possible, their assessment of the people in your team. You can also gather the support and resources that they can provide. It is also useful to find out their existing talent development framework and processes so that you can work hand-in-glove with them. Ensuring you are aligned with HR's overall talent development plan is critical as it makes it easy for them to give you their full commitment as your plan is in agreement with their bigger scheme.

- Your people: These are your most important stakeholders. You should know their career aspiration, their strengths and growth areas. As their immediate supervisor, these factors provide essential information that you must be familiar with, as you support their well-being, performance and future success. Hold one-on-one conversations with each one of them to re-ascertain their wants, needs, expectations, aspirations and even their fears. Then make sure to follow-up with each person. Adam, a manager whom we know from our coaching work, conducts "1:1 coffee chats" once every three to four months with each individual direct report. He made clear to his people that the coffee chats are all about them — getting to know their aspiration, learning and growth needs and what are needed to make their job even more satisfying, meaningful and impactful for them. Adam had previously tried to save time by having a group coffee chat, but he found people were not as open talking about their inner hopes and concerns when their colleagues were at the same meeting. The one-on-one environment offers the necessary psychological safety and a warm space for heart-to-heart talks.

b. Discipline of Collaborate

With the information collected, you can have a sense of where your team members are in terms of their performance, potentials and aspirations. As shown in Figure 13-2, you can use McKinsey's 9-box Performance and Potential Grid to add structure to your thought process:

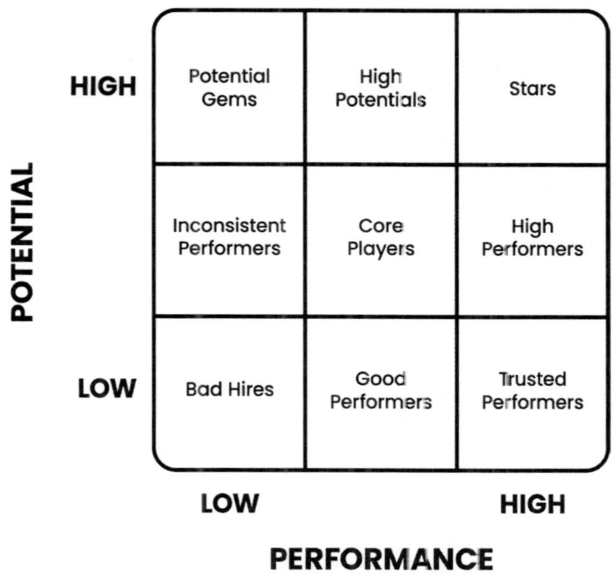

Figure 13-2: 9-Box Performance & Potential Grid

This grid enables you to have a clear view of where your team members are before you dive into co-creating the individual plans for, and with each of them. The grid helps you to be fairer and more objective in the way you evaluate your people's contributions and future potential, relative to each other.

One way to ***collaborate*** is to involve your boss and HR with a blank page. Using a blank 9-Grid chart, you engage your boss and HR to collectively decide where to place each of your team members in the grid. Building the picture from scratch is advantageous as everyone at the table has equal opportunity and voice to shape the eventual outputs.

Another method, which takes lesser time, is for you to pre-fill the boxes as "preliminary inputs". You will then use the meeting to obtain validation and confirmation from your boss and HR of your assessment. The advantage is you have the first opportunity to place your people and this puts you in better control. The disadvantage is there may be less involvement from your boss and HR. In this case, you need to intentionally let them do more talking and a good way is to ask more questions to draw out their views and support.

With the agreement from your boss and HR on the 9-box grid, you can then confidently deep dive into the Individual Growth Plans (IGP). It is important that each IGP be co-owned with your individual team members. The IGPs will fail if your members do not own them. Have a 1:1 conversation with each of them, asking them to reflect and share their thoughts to questions such as:

- "What is my career goal?"
- "What are the growth areas that I need for my current and future roles?"
- "Why is it important to me that I grow these areas?"
- "How can I develop these areas?"
- "What outcomes do I want to see?"

c. Discipline of Challenge

In the process of the collaborative discussions, you will have ample opportunities to create the space for the discipline of ***challenge*** to take place. Challenge can take the following forms:

i. Challenge each other's views

In all your meetings, whether with your boss or HR, or with your people, you want open and candid discussions on areas such as their contributions, performance, strengths, potential, weaknesses and their growth needs. There may be disagreements and concerns, which you will do well to hear them out as early as possible. Taking the time and open attitude to listen to opposing views or adverse feedback is one of the hallmarks of a Shared Leader. Your readiness to listen will encourage people you work with to speak their minds. Several references are made in the Bible of King Solomon, one of the wisest leaders, who exhorted the readers to seek wise counsel. Because you welcome and are open to be challenged and to be influenced by others, you have not only created a safe and trusting environment of openness and candor but have also provided your colleagues with good role modeling that they can follow.

In the wise words of Mr. Yuen Kuan Moo, the Group CEO of Singtel, one of the largest telco in Asia, who said this in a leadership seminar: "When you create an environment where people are allowed or willing to speak up and not just defer to authority, you will see a lot of natural leaders emerging because they no longer have that fear of just listening to the boss, no longer have that constraint that I am just going to deliver that order, but I am coming up the solution. I think this is where leaders need to be changing their style, even if they know the subject. *I would encourage leaders to be patient, to hear someone out first before you put in the judgement or comment because the last thing you want is to shut people off and send the wrong message to the larger group.* Leaders cast a long shadow.

How you behave is not only to the person that you are talking to, but the rest of the people who are watching".

ii. Challenge everyone's personal and professional comfort zone

You want everyone to challenge themselves, to think big, to think of how the strategic future will look like to them, and the new possibilities that they can have. You want them to own their career growth. For example, one of our coaches was coaching a senior manager from a global consulting firm. She was a key talent who was able to help her boss achieve a steady stream of strong revenues by designing winning client proposals. Her immediate career goal was to be promoted to Managing Director. But she was not perceived to be highly collaborative and at the same time, she was also neglecting her physical health. She could work like a machine, going for hours without food or rest. The coach challenged her by helping her visualize her future and what wholesome success would look like to her. She recognized and accepted that if she was to continue the current work pattern, her career, and even her life, ran the risk of being derailed.

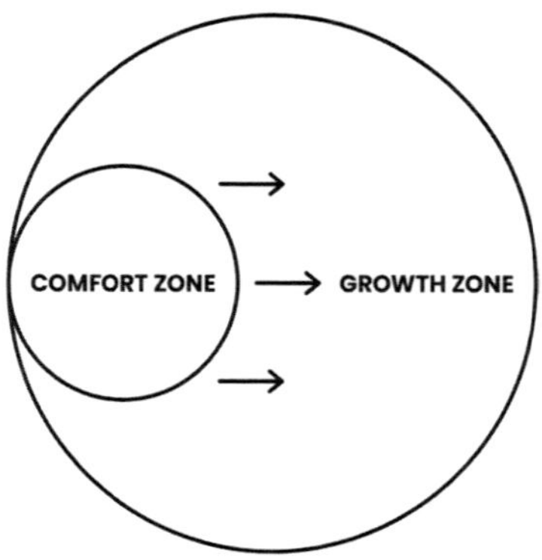

Figure 13-3: From Comfort Zone To Growth

Our coaches have worked with numerous clients on their growth areas. These growth areas are listed in Table 13-1. They are not exhaustive, but one where you may be able to identify the growth areas for your team members with the help of tools such as the 360-degree feedback.

1	Increasing executive presence & visibility
2	Developing ability to think strategically
3	Becoming better at sharing leadership with peers and team members
4	Developing higher business or commercial acumen
5	Becoming a more confident public speaker
6	Becoming better at managing bosses and upper stakeholders
7	Influencing peers and colleagues without authority
8	Be more assertive and meeting own professional and personal needs
9	Reducing over-thinking, increase self-confidence and speak up more freely
10	Becoming more effective and quicker at making decisions
11	Delegating more and holding others accountable
12	Preparing for bigger job responsibilities or new job roles
13	Building a higher performance, shared leadership culture in my team
14	Becoming a more inspiring, engaging and motivating leader
15	Managing change and projects with good alignment and buy-in
16	Building trust faster and better in my team and with colleagues
17	Become more effective in holding meetings that are engaging, productive and fun
18	Improving my negotiation skills with internal and / or with external stakeholders
19	Connecting, socializing and creating more fun in my team
20	Becoming a more authentic, empathetic and caring leader
21	Incorporating more coaching in my leadership style
22	Becoming more effective in conducting difficult feedback conversations
23	Conducting performance appraisal and feedback conversations
24	Better at leading and coaching low performers in my team
25	Developing a player and growth mindset
26	Better at managing my emotions & have more self-compassion
27	Developing greater resilience to cope with work challenges
28	Becoming better focused, better at setting priorities and managing time
29	Better at balancing work, family and personal life
30	Improving my physical and mental health (including sleep, nutrition, exercise & rest)

Table 13-1: Possible Growth Areas for Leaders

iii. Challenge organizational boundaries

Organizations and teams have "invisible" boundaries. There are unspoken limitations that everyone seemingly or habitually accepts. Siva was a team supervisor who had a hard time managing 21 team members for the past two years. Even though the 21 team members were split into 4 teams, he still spent an inordinate amount of time conducting four weekly team meetings and handling their individual issues. When our coach asked him about his delegation, his reply was that he could not do much delegation as in the company structure, they do not have "team lead" positions. He believed that he was not able to appoint team leads as it would mean a promotion for them, resulting in higher salary costs. After challenging his assumptions, he eventually realized that for each of the 4 teams, he could assign one team member to the role of "Team Lead" and positioned it as a learning opportunity. In fact, his eventual plan was to rotate the team lead roles so that more team members have a chance to learn. Every organization has boundaries or internal processes in place. With due respect, you can still challenge and push these boundaries, either by highlighting the need to change, or like Siva, to find creative solutions and not be hampered by it.

Powerful questions that you can ask to challenge the status quo include:

- "What is blocking us from achieving our goal?"
- "How can we accelerate the learning and growth of the team?"
- "If we designed from scratch with no baggage or constraints, how would we do it?"

d. Discipline of Contract

Good work! By this stage you will have an overview of where your team members are in the 9-box grid and you also have a concrete IGP, customized for each team member. Using the disciplines of Collaborate and Challenge, these plans are co-created with the pushing of envelopes to get the best out of everyone's potential. With their involvement as co-designers and co-creators, your team members will have more reasons and motivation to want to implement their IGP successfully.

But simply completing your members' IGPs is not enough. It is essential to gain commitment and establish accountability from the key people. There are two levels of contracting that you need to do.

i. Contracting with your boss and HR. The first level is with your boss and HR for specific support and resources to ensure the IGPs can be properly implemented and fulfilled. One important action is to organize a meeting with your boss and HR to ensure alignment on key questions such as:

- Why are the IGPs important to the team and the organization?
- What is the impact on the team and organization when the IGPs are successfully implemented?
- What specific support and resources are needed from the boss and HR to implement the IGP?

ii. Contracting with your team. The second level of contracting is with your team members. Knowing the specific support and resources that you have from the first meeting will allow you to make concrete offers and at the same time, obtain their commitment. Your 1:1 conversation with each of them should include:

- Alignment of the outcomes and expectations
- Your offer to them, including specific resources and support (that you have obtained from the boss and HR)
- Asking them for their requests
- Agree on follow up meetings to measure progress and check accountability

As you can see from the above process, ***contracting*** is a carefully thought-out and planned approach. The real journey needs to start well. Every person that matters in the entire process needs to be involved, aligned and committed. The key is your ability to dive into and get commitment on the specifics. Failure in the implementation is usually caused by the lack of clear contracting. Anyone in the "right" frame of mind will certainly express support for a noble scheme such as the IGPs. But will the same person be committed to spend time to have tea or have regular mentoring sessions with your people? Or will HR or Finance be willing to budget sufficient money to support the IGPs?

The discipline of contracting is on-going. It needs to start at the beginning of the program and during the implementation, you will review, get feedback and make adjustments to the plans. This flexibility is good as there is no perfect plan. After each adjustment, there should be clear re-contracting so that everyone remains clear on their commitment and accountability. It should not take long. The process of contracting will leave no doubt in anyone's mind who is doing what, by when and very importantly, how success will be measured.

e. Discipline of Connect

In this chapter, while the discipline of ***Connect*** is described last, it does not mean it is the least important. "Connect" happens throughout the entire process as you will actively engage the stakeholders with the aim to know them better at the personal dimension. This will help build greater trust and closer relationships over time, creating openness and transparency as everyone feels the psychological safety to share their inner voices with you and with each other. The discipline of Connect also includes helping your stakeholders connect at the systemic level. They will see how your plans tie in with your team, the entire organization and the business. The ambience and relationships that you have created with them makes your and everyone's work more meaningful and more fun.

So What? ...... Insights

Each year, organizations collectively spend billions on developing their people. Conventional wisdom holds that if you develop your people, they will help you to develop your business. People also want to learn and grow in their work, and by ensuring this happens it becomes a Win-Win situation leading to increased employee engagement. But it won't just happen. It requires constant attention, effort and commitment.

The answer to people development is within the team. Help your people learn and grow while they work. When you share your leadership with your people, their learning will accelerate. To quote Ralph Emerson: "Skills to do come of doing".

The 5 disciplines are a very effective framework to plan and manage the development of your people. It is a partnership approach. Using Connect, Contract, Collect, Collaborate and Challenge will enable a higher level of ownership, concrete commitment and mutual accountability to the development of your people. When you are able to accelerate the real growth of your people, your organization and business will also enjoy accelerated real growth as well. Learning and earning must be inseparable.

Learning and earning must be inseparable.

Creating A Shared Leadership Culture

"The best way to predict the future is to create it."

Abraham Lincoln
16th U.S. President

Organizational culture is the collective way of how team members in your organization think, behave, interact and perform. "The way things are done here" is influenced by the prevailing mindsets, values, beliefs, norms, behaviors and expectations.

Most of us have experienced the real impact that culture has on ourselves and our team's performance. According to a report by Human Synergistics International (HSI), an American organization that specializes in understanding and measuring thinking and behavioral styles since the early 1970s, 84% of leaders believe culture is important to business success. Tellingly, 60% of these same leaders believe culture is more important than the business strategy or operating models.

Other studies have shown the direct correlation between leadership, performance and culture. In a research study of 114 leaders of technology companies published by the Journal of Applied Psychology of the American Psychology Association in 2016, it was found that CEOs who challenged the existing cultural norms of their organizations improved their financial results and were able to implement fresh strategies. These CEOs also achieved an increase in return on their assets of 1% to 4% within the first year.

Where does our organizational culture come from?

An organization's culture can be likened to an iceberg, with both visible and invisible aspects. The visible section "above the water line" refers to the behaviors that everyone can observe and experience — how we really live, act, treat each other and work. It includes the way problems are discussed, decisions made and what & how information is communicated. It also includes the type of stories, jokes and gossips that are shared among the management and the employees.

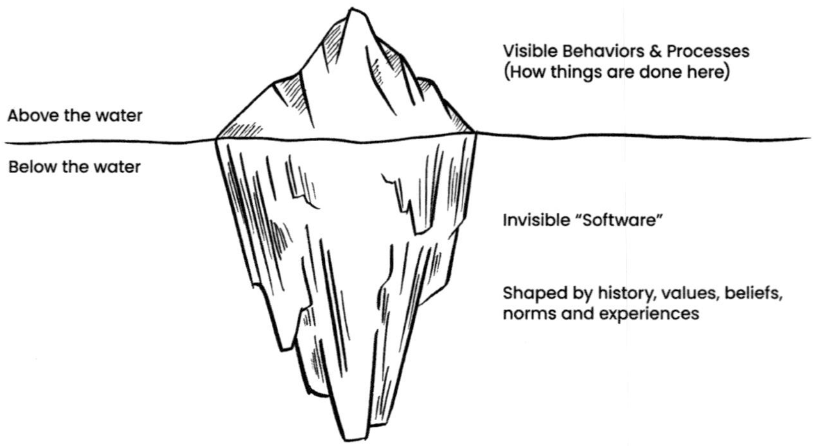

Figure 14-1: Organizational Culture

The much larger part of the iceberg, hidden from public view, contains the "software" that influences and drives the actual behaviors and attitudes. It is influenced and molded by factors such as the history, values, beliefs, norms and experiences that are shared by the leaders and members. In addition to these factors, leaders especially in global organizations, must also consider how both national cultures and industry cultures can have an impact on their organizations and strategies.

Intentional versus Incidental

As an organization's culture is essential to its performance and sustainability, it is paramount for leaders to take control and intentionally shape that culture. Leaving the organization to incidentally or accidentally determine and form its own culture is not strategic leadership. To be strategic is to lead the present with the future clearly in mind. Thomas Frey, a futurist said it well: "*The future creates the present*". We should thus be spending time in the present to intentionally shape our desired future culture. The logic is clear. By the time we reach the point in the future, we should have the culture that we need. Our culture should lead and support, and not lag or be a drag on the organization. To intentionally shape the organizational culture, leaders must have a good game plan to actively seek to improve the whole iceberg, working on both the visible as well as its submerged "operating" software.

Thomas Frey, a futurist said it well: "The future creates the present". We should thus be spending time in the present to intentionally shape our desired future culture.

Foundational pillars of your culture

Culture is not static. It is dynamic. It flows with the times. As culture is "alive" and evolving, it is therefore important to have your organizational culture to be based on solid and enduring foundational pillars. Without the foundational pillars, you will have a harder time to adjust and improve your culture.

Anyone who has tried to implement a culture change program will know the amount of work that is needed, including overcoming all sorts of pushback and resistance. McKinsey has reported that 70% of change initiatives do not achieve their intended objectives. It is no wonder that many leaders are usually apprehensive when culture change is proposed, for it is likely they have experienced their fair share of failed interventions.

If culture is to be kept relevant with the changing environment, it must be capable of continuously evolving, adapting and renewing. It is like a building with strong foundational pillars. The solid pillars allow the building to be renovated, overhauled and re-purposed, without causing its core to be shaken. In Singapore, the Old Supreme Court Building was built in 1937 and had been overhauled and re-purposed from being the highest courthouse of the country to becoming the National Art Gallery. It still is the most handsome and majestic of the historic buildings in Singapore, despite undergoing major interior and exterior changes in the last 80 years. Judging from the past track records, we can safely say that in the future, this grand lady in Singapore will continue to stand firmly, even if it is to undergo future rounds of renewal.

The 5 Shared Leadership Disciplines® will make solid foundational pillars for any high performing culture. Here are the reasons why:

1. The Pillar of Connect

A foundational pillar where members develop their personal associations with each other, and their connectedness with the purpose, mission and vision of the organization and team. Strong connectedness, relationships and having a high sense of belonging are the foundation of every high performing culture.

2. The Pillar of Contract

Members actively seek understanding and teamwork through ensuring alignment, agreement and commitment in their roles, responsibilities, goals, outcomes and work, with and among each other. Members are 100% responsible for what needs to be achieved. They hold themselves and each other accountable to do what they agreed to do.

3. The Pillar of Collect

Members proactively seek and collect wisdom from others. This wisdom includes thoughts, ideas, feelings, experiences and tacit knowledge that others have. Everyone respects and values inputs and inclusivity. The openness to "collect", and the readiness to listen, demonstrate humility and honesty that one does not know everything. This openness to listen and learn is another hallmark of a high performing culture.

4. The Pillar of Collaboration

Having a foundational pillar of collaboration means solutions are often actively co-designed and co-created with the involvement of the right people at the right time. This ensures a high sense of ownership, commitment and positive energy which are critical for implementation success. The ability, ease and speed of collaborating within the team and with other teams, both vertically and laterally across the organization, is dependent on the strength of this pillar.

This will help bridge the many silos that are prevalent in many organizations and teams.

5. The Pillar of Challenge

Members feel psychologically safe and free to speak up, challenge and influence each other with their thoughts, feelings and actions relating to any aspects of the Business, Organization, Team, Professional, Personal and Sustainability dimensions. In turn, each person is open to be challenged and influenced by others, demonstrate their vulnerability and go outside their comfort zone.

When a culture is built using the 5 Shared Leadership Disciplines® as foundational pillars, you can expect three major competitive advantages:

- The collective capability and capacity of the team is significantly higher than that of a single leader. The organization that can harness its total energy and resources will be ahead in the marketplace.
- The open, safe and free environment created by the 5 disciplines will bring out the best of everyone -- junior and senior team members alike. Members will readily speak up, step up and proactively take more ownership and leadership to achieve the team and organizational goals.
- The speed of change will be faster as the 5 disciplines create more adaptability and nimbleness in the members, team and the organization.

How to create the culture we want

Chapter 10 describes how we can use Shared Leadership Disciplines® to plan and implement change. In this chapter, we will continue to discuss change, focusing specifically on a very frequently-asked question: "How do I implement shared leadership culture in my team or organization?"

To implement change, Kurt Lewin, the German-born psychologist, offers a simple, yet powerful process. He likened it to changing the shape of an ice-cube. You cannot simply force a solid cube-shaped piece of ice to make it cylindrical in shape. The ice will break. You would first need to melt the cube-shaped ice to water and then refreeze the melted water in a cylindrical ice-making mold. His 3-step change process is as follows:

Step 1: Unfreeze

Before you implement change, you need to have your key people accept the need for change. This requires building relationships and trust. It is also important to have the right conversations with the people involved or affected by the change. The conversations will cover what, why and how the change might be carried out and the impact or the "so what" of the change.

Step 2: Change

The next stage is to plan and implement the change. It involves equipping people with new skills and supporting them with the new attitudes and behaviors. Communication, feedback and evaluating progress are important elements needed throughout the change process.

Step 3: Re-freeze

The third stage is to consolidate the change so that it is now the new normal. It includes bolstering the new behaviors using positive reinforcement measures such as recognition and rewards, adjusting the performance management system, continuing to train people in the new behaviors, hiring people with these new attitudes and behaviors, and integrating the change into procedures and policies.

In the following sections, we will discuss how you can shape the culture of your team and what you can do to change the culture of a large organization.

How to shape your team culture

When you are directly in charge of your team, this is probably your best opportunity to shape or influence the culture of your team using the 5 Shared Leadership Disciplines® as your foundation.

1. Connect

Build closer relationship with the team members by getting to know them at the personal level. Create opportunities for team members to learn more about each other, from personal interests, to family, to their professional aspirations.

2. Collect

Gather information from the team relating to what is working and what needs changing in the current culture. Ask them for their hopes and expectations in a future culture. Do the same with other stakeholders who have working knowledge of your team. Collect and review data from Employee Satisfaction Surveys relating to your leadership and the team. Conduct a focused feedback survey with your team members using a combination of questionnaires, 1:1 conversations and focused groups. The process of collecting will serve to strengthen your change plan.

When you are directly in charge of your team, this is probably your best opportunity to shape or influence the culture of your team using the 5 Shared Leadership Disciplines® as your foundation.

3. Collaborate

Involve every team member to co-design, co-create and co-own the culture. It is best to state the culture attributes in actionable terms so that everyone is able to implement them. Everyone in the team is capable of role-modeling for each other, especially when there is high acceptance and ownership. Culture is caught, not taught. One important step is to jointly develop a set of team norms that everyone in the team can commit to.

4. Challenge

In conjunction with "collaborate", challenge the team to think outside their comfort zones by specifying aspects of culture that could prove valuable to the team now, and in the future. As an example, we work with teams that specify that they must adopt norms that include "speak up with good intent", "keep an open mind" or "step out of comfort zone".

5. Contract

When the vision of the future team culture is clear and accepted by the whole team, you will have achieved alignment. What is now needed is to gain the commitment from each team member to implement the norms consciously and conscientiously. One way to do so is to hold everyone accountable for implementation of the norms and agreeing on when and how progress will be measured.

The "Connect" and "Collect" disciplines are equivalent to the Unfreezing stage of the Kurt Lewin's Model. The "Collaborate" and "Challenge" is the Change stage and the "Contract" is the Re-freezing stage.

The 5 Shared Leadership Disciplines® are not a one-way or one-cycle process. Neither is there a single pathway to creating the culture you want. The "Connect" is implemented at the beginning as it is so essential to relate at the personal level for the latter part to be done well. The other Disciplines are implemented according to the "who" and the "context" of the team, depending on the current culture and the readiness and urgency to change. Other factors include the personalities, maturity and competency of the team members.

The above sequence works for both new teams or a team where the leader and members know each other well. The variable is the pace needed for each of the process. The leader has to implement at a speed and time that all members can and will support. The adage "Slow is Fast" holds true, especially when trying to change a deep-rooted culture.

How can we create a shared leadership culture in a large organization?

There are two approaches to creating a shared leadership culture in a large organization:

Top down with the senior leadership

Typically, senior leadership provides the mandate, sponsorship and resources to start and implement a major change. When a Senior Leadership Team (SLT) leads by example, the rest of the organization will follow. There are key things you can do to get the top leadership approval:

1. Make a compelling organizational or business case

- You have to create a compelling organizational or business case for the change. Collect data on incidents, employee survey outcomes, employee exit reports or feedback that show inherent cultural weaknesses that need to be tackled. Explain the negative impact on the organization if the culture is not improved. Create a sense of urgency. One way is to show the current culture is not fully aligned or supporting the strategic vision or direction of the organization. Another way is to compare and benchmark your culture with other players and competitors in the industry. Make a case that to stay abreast or ahead of the curve, culture 2.0 is needed.

2. Provide senior management the Shared Leadership Discipline experiences

- **Facilitated workshop**
  Organize a face-to-face or virtual workshop that allows the SLT to experience first-hand how the 5 Shared Leadership Disciplines and the Action Reflection Learning principles and tools address real challenges and opportunities facing them.

- **Just-In-Time coaching intervention**
  Another opportunity for experiential learning would be to use Shared Leadership Disciplines and the Action Reflection Learning tools just in time, when the SLT needs it. This could be during a difficult meeting moment where the use of the ARL tools will enable them to get unstuck and experience a breakthrough. For just-in-time coaching to work, it would require at least one member of the SLT to be trained and equipped with the Shared Leadership Team Coaching tool kit. Alternatively, the SLT can invite a team coach to observe their deliberations and to jump in with a just-in-time learning moment when the need arises.

3. Learn from qualified Shared Leadership Coaches

- Invite your CEO and key members of the SLT to learn and experience Shared Leadership at an external forum or webinar. There is good value learning from external coaches as they would be able to bring their wide and varied experiences to the room. At such events, your CEO and SLT can also learn from the leaders of other organizations about their shared leadership experiences and journey.

4. Find an influential advocate

- As you may not be a member of the SLT, having an advocate who is a full and regular member of the SLT can be helpful to lobby for you. Your advocate can be your department head, mentor or anyone who is already on board with you. A respected and influential advocate will add weight to your case during the management discussions and will also help you address difficult questions on your behalf and direct the SLT's thinking.

- Besides having a main advocate at the SLT level, it is also very useful to cultivate other advocates from within the SLT and the leadership level immediately below the SLT. These advocates may not be in the meeting room with you, but you can certainly bring their "voice" to the room through their testimonials and successes.

Getting the top leadership approval is by far the optimum approach. This allows the senior leaders to take the lead and show the way, ensuring a higher chance of successfully shaping the organizational culture. If these senior leaders experience and commit to practicing the 5 disciplines, they can shape a shared leadership culture by living it. Then it would only be natural for them to cascade the 5 disciplines to their own teams and down the line until the entire organization is living and breathing a shared leadership culture.

Bottom-up from the team level

Another practical approach is to start at the team level and let it percolate upwards to the SLT. A good starting point is to create a core group of internal Shared Leadership Team Coaches. This group consists of a mix of line leaders and HR. This core team will develop themselves to become competent, confident, and credible team coaches who, being insiders, can be the catalysts to make Shared Leadership "come alive". This core group will be able to do several things:

1. Expand the base

- The core group can create and implement shared leadership development programs to expand the base of team leaders with the required skills and have them practice with their teams over a period of a few weeks or months. Adding progress checks, measurements and mentoring to the program will create even more impact. The positive impact and feedback from the teams provide valuable ground evidence to convince the SLT to embrace shared leadership.

2. Expand the advocates and champions

- Expanding the number of advocates and champions across the organization will help spread the word about the importance of the change effort. These advocates and champions will be team leaders who themselves have experienced sharing their leadership and are now converts. They will be your best champions and role models. Better still, support the growth of these advocates and champions by helping them to be fully certified as Shared Leadership Team Coaches. This way the core group will have more trained resources to create even more success.

3. Expand the experience

- Have a few of your passionate supporters and advocates to implement Shared Leadership Disciplines in their departments or teams. Support them and help them with the implementation, including equipping their team members with the skills. Measure their results, collect their feedback and evaluate their impact. The data from the pilot will help you in your business case.

4. Expand the testimonials

- Communicating success is key to garnering more interest and ensuring the message is positively lodged in the employees' minds. Success stories and testimonials can include both the qualitative and quantitative impact that embracing Shared Leadership Disciplines has on them. The success stories and testimonials can be compiled and creatively presented in the organization's various employee communication channels. This can also reinforce the business case for change.

Below are additional pointers to note:

1. Build on what has already been laid

- While you want to make sharing leadership an alternative way to lead, it is by no means exclusive. It can be viewed as an underlay, that is, a base or foundation layer where the existing culture and leadership styles can be built upon. For example, a team or organization that has or is building a coaching culture can implement Shared Leadership as the foundation to reinforce and strengthen that culture.

2. Find the opportunities to experience Shared Leadership

- Shared Leadership Disciplines and Action Reflection Learning principles and tools are best learned through relevant experience such as when solving their real challenges and issues. Therefore, the question on your mind is "Where and when are the good opportunities for the leaders to experience Shared Leadership in action?"

3. Select the right departments or teams to start

- In a large organization, there will be several departments and teams to choose from. Choosing the right departments or teams to start is critical. One important selection criterion is the commitment and enthusiasm of the department and team leaders. Their commitment and enthusiasm will result in being open-minded, keen to learn and willing to try new things and to persevere in the journey. These are essential elements for a successful pilot.

4. Allow the roots to grow deep

- It is important to nurture and nourish the team leaders and their members over a period of time to ensure new habits and norms take root. Only then can you expect to see the fruits. Shared leadership can be implemented in stages. Allowing sufficient time for the core team to work with the team leaders and teams will ensure sharing leadership has taken root. If you move too fast, there is a risk that the roots are not firmly grounded in the soil and before long, it gets uprooted by some other events or corporate initiatives.

5. Measure the progress

- Measuring the progress of change, both qualitatively and quantitatively, will provide the focus and motivation to the leaders and advocates. Remember "what gets measured gets done". It is also important to continually acknowledge the people who are leading and supporting the change. "What gets recognized gets repeated". Celebrate the success, be it big or small achievements. Results can also be reported to the SLT regularly. At some point, the SLT will take note of the impact that Shared Leadership has at the team level, and will be convinced about embracing the sharing of leadership as a new culture of leading and being.

So What? ...... Insights

Culture has a major impact on our people, performance, organization and the business. The kind of culture we want cannot be left to incidental formation. A more intentional approach is needed to proactively shape the culture. The 5 Shared Leadership Disciplines® can be the strong foundational pillars in which to develop and shape the culture you need — now and into the future.

The bottom line is:

- Be clear with the "Why" and develop advocates and champions for change
- Bring the leaders on board to co-create & co-own the change
- Have a clear blueprint for implementation and communication
- Keep the focus, measure the progress and use the results to inspire for more
- Practice what you preach, for culture is caught, not taught
- Recognize & celebrate every achievement, big or small
- Persevere and be patient. You, together with all involved, will see and enjoy the fruits of the new culture

CHAPTER 15

Sustainability — A Strategic Priority

We have invited Isabel Rimanoczy, a former LIM partner and opinion leader in the field of sustainability mindset, to write this chapter on 'Sustainability, a Strategic Priority'. Developing a sustainability mindset is the responsibility and opportunity for all leaders and coaches. This chapter will enable us to discover what more we can do, both as leaders and coaches to make Sustainability a strategic priority. – The Authors

---

"We have to do both: to figure out how to integrate the sustainability mindset into a curriculum while we teach net present value, your standard balance sheet items or supply and demand."

Professor Ilian Mihov
Dean of INSEAD Business School, Fontainebleau, France

Chapter 12 introduced the importance of sustainability from two perspectives:

1. The sustainability of the planet
2. The sustainability of the organization

The detailed exploration of the VUCA characteristics of our contemporary world highlighted the importance of adopting leadership practices that address the volatile, uncertain, complex and ambiguous times. The context of the exploration was the sustainability of the organization.

In this chapter the focus will be on the other perspective of sustainability, the broader one related to the planet. While this differentiation is useful in some instances, it can lead to the misconception that both perspectives can be dealt with independently.

In a conversation with the dean of a Business School in Shanghai several years ago, the dean reflected on a presentation about the planetary sustainability challenges, stating, "We don't have the luxury to think of the planet; we need to focus on business first!" Certainly, he would think differently today, as we have all become more aware of the interconnectedness of both aspects. It may be easier to conceptualize and strategize how to implement sustainable practices within a single organization, but the reality is that unless humans concern themselves with our planet's fragility, there is no business. Given the disruption to supply chains caused by tsunamis, droughts, floods, pandemics, social unrest, and various conflicts and wars, business profitability is directly and deeply impacted and can no longer be seen as the highest priority.

The right mindset

The year 2005 brought a significant milestone in the understanding of our planet's challenges, with the movie "An Inconvenient Truth", and the Nobel Peace Prize was awarded to US Vice-president Al Gore. Around that same time, I initiated my doctoral research at Columbia University, Teachers College, New York, to delve into the potential impact of business leaders on sustainability. Specifically, I explored the learning processes and motivations of business leaders who had championed initiatives that have had a positive impact on the planet or the community. I focused on identifying if there were some aspects, whether knowledge or ways of thinking, that could be intentionally developed, in order to shape a generation of social and environmentally responsible leaders (Rimanoczy, 2010[i]).

The findings of this qualitative exploratory study pointed to a series of aspects that related to the thinking (how the leaders thought, processed and interpreted information), and to the being (their values, their sense of oneness with nature and their sense of purpose). I identified those aspects that were integral to the achievement of positive sustainability results and lent themselves to intentional educational development programs.

With this new framework, I was invited to design a course to develop the sustainability mindset for students at the Masters of Hospitality and Tourism, Fairleigh Dickinson University, New Jersey (Rimanoczy, 2013[ii]) The results were extraordinary. Developing those aspects had a transformative impact on how the students saw themselves, each other, and the world, with a direct consequence on their habits and behaviors. Further iterations of this program, replicated at other business schools (Fordham University, NY; Nova Southeastern University, Florida; Kingston University, UK; Universidad de Navarra, Spain; Al-Akhawayn University, Morocco) created the foundation for a movement of higher education professors from more than 220 universities and business schools in 57 countries. They have been collaborating to develop a sustainability mindset through their teaching. The stories of mind-shift, described by the professors and through the words of the students have been recently published in the book *Revolutionizing Sustainability Education: Tools and stories of mindset transformation* (Ivanova & Rimanoczy, 2022[iii]).

What is a Sustainability Mindset?

In the previous chapter the image of an iceberg was used as an analogy to describe organizational culture. The business decisions and processes are the visible section of the iceberg, while the section underwater represents the components of the corporate culture: values, vision, priorities, and tacit beliefs that shape and condition the visible behaviors.

We can use the same image of the iceberg to describe the sustainability mindset of an individual. Above the water surface, we observe behaviors, decisions and choices the individual makes. Under the water lie hidden the foundation of values, beliefs, assumptions, and ways to process information, which shape and condition the visible behaviors. The Sustainability Mindset is a particular way of thinking and being that puts the planet first.

Here is an example. A VP of Marketing is hard pressed to take a decision because she just found out that their main competitor is about to launch a product very similar to one her company has been developing. Her product is not ready to be launched, since the manufacturing director required more time to fix some random errors found in the testing phase. But after such a large financial investment in the R&D of her product, the prospect of missing the 'first-come' advantage in the market is not something she wants to risk. She decides to authorize the launch, taking the responsibility for any malfunctions that might occur. "Things can be fixed later, when (and if) they happen."

The Sustainability Mindset is a particular way of thinking and being that puts the planet first.

In this example the mindset shaping the decision shows the VP's short-term thinking, a dualistic logic (either we win being first to market, or we lose); a fragmented vision of information (focusing on the launch, and postponing considerations related to problems for the buyer, potential brand damage, lawsuits, insurance consequences etc.). Other "underwater" aspects shaping her decision were her personal sense of pace (act quickly, don't spend more time analyzing assumptions or stakeholder views); and perhaps some identity factors (a wish to be seen as assertive, action-oriented and decisive, rather than hesitant or "soft").

The rushed launch may have other consequences, such as a failure to think through the need for disposal of pollutants related to the product, questionable packaging that may create unnecessary waste, perhaps even undisclosed (unregulated) health implications for the user. This happens all the time!

The Sustainability Mindset is described in 12 Principles (see Figure 15-1). The principles fall into four content areas: Ecological Worldview, Systems Perspective, Emotional Intelligence and Spiritual Intelligence (Rimanoczy, 2021[iv]).

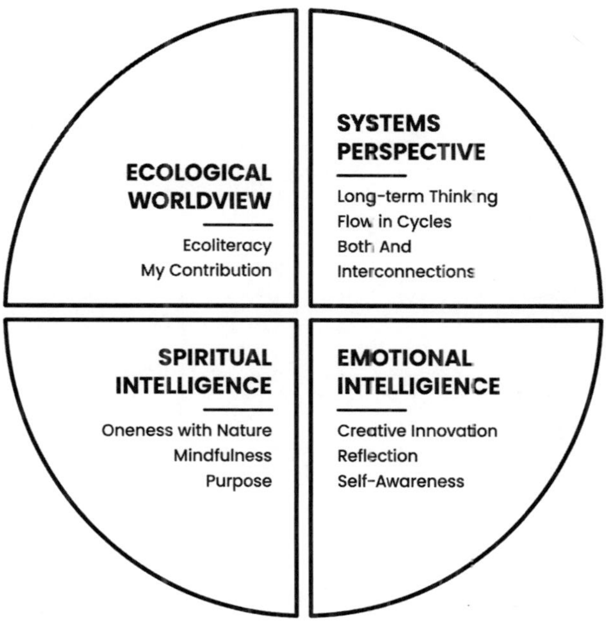

Figure 15-1: The 12 Sustainability Mindset Principles And The 4 Content Areas

Why does it matter?

When we take a closer look at the unsustainable problems we are facing, we can quickly recognize that many are direct or indirect consequences of human behaviors – which, in turn, are the result of our values, beliefs and assumptions (our mindset).

Problem	Behaviors causing the problem	Underlying mindset
Flooding and landslides forcing evacuations and property loss	Deforestation practices. Clear-cutting of forest to gain land for cattle or profitable, in-demand monocultures (i.e. soy, corn, palm oil).	Short-term thinking Dualistic thinking (I win or I lose) Not my problem
Plastic in waterways; micro-plastics entering the food chain via seafood with uncertain health implications; cost of clean-up; impact on tourism and economic loss	Production of plastic containers, packaging, components and products; disposal practices and poor waste management	Short-term thinking Comfort provided by new products Innovation is the priority Don't see interconnections Focus on growth and profits
Biodiversity loss, species extinction, uncertain implications.	Urban sprawl. Poor land management. Development of natural areas. Construction of dams, highways. Relocation of inhabitants.	Rapid decisions Short-term thinking Priority given to growth and profits Trust human ingenuity to address consequences Technology trumps nature

Table 15-1: The unsustainable problems

How can we develop a Sustainability Mindset?

The twelve Principles provide a framework to notice our thinking patterns and habits, and to develop a Sustainability Mindset.

Within the **Ecological Worldview** there are two principles:

1. **Ecoliteracy:** Understanding the state of the planet allows us to be more fully aware of the challenges, the complexity of how

these are linked to each other, and to explore what it means to us.

2. **My contribution:** When we identify the ways in which we are unintentionally contributing to the problems, we have a chance to do something about them. It also expands our consciousness and develops social sensitivity.

Within **Systems Perspective** there are four principles:

3. **Long term thinking:** Every action has consequences that are not immediately visible. However, short-term thinking is most frequently prioritized, at the expense of exploring the long-term consequences of our business decisions. Therefore, balancing the two perspectives considering also the long-term when analyzing situations and making decisions has a positive impact on global sustainability.
4. **Both Plus / And thinking:** We are experiencing the impact of a polarized world, based on 'either/or' thinking. Both "+ and" thinking allows us to understand paradoxes and calls for creative solutions that are inclusive of all stakeholders.
5. **Flow in cycles:** There are no linear processes in Nature: Everything flows in cycles of birth, growth, death, and rebirth. Many aspects of man-made unsustainability of the planet are a result of the misconception that we are not governed by this law of Nature.
6. **Interconnectedness:** When we see interconnectedness, we understand the importance of diversity, and our decisions and actions become more inclusive, which contributes to the sustainability of the whole.

Within the content area of **Emotional Intelligence** there are three Principles:

7. **Reflection:** Reflective practices help to pause, and to ponder the situation and its implications before jumping into action.

8. **Self-awareness:** When we explore our personal values, beliefs, assumptions, and motivations, we gain greater control over our actions, and we can see new alternative behaviors.
9. **Creative innovation:** Resilience is based on constant creativity, innovation and experimentation. When we neglect the non-rational wisdom we have in us, our solutions are missing critical information, and may create negative impacts on the ecosystem and society.

There are three Principles within the content area of **Spiritual Intelligence:**

10. **Oneness with nature:** Understanding that we are one with Nature, a species within species, is a powerful spiritual experience that can shape behaviors leading to a more harmonious relationship with each other and all beings.
11. **Mindfulness:** Mindfulness is being fully present, experiencing connectedness with all that is. Mindfulness enhances awareness and compassion and predisposes one to social and environmental actions.
12. **Purpose:** Defining our purpose provides an unconscious compass, and when it is grounded in values of our higher self, we actively shape a better world.

These principles provide a scaffolding to address the complexity of a mindset. They are certainly not the only components of a mindset, yet they have been proven to be easy paths to prompt a mindset-shift.

These principles provide a scaffolding to address the complexity of a mindset. They are certainly not the only components of a mindset, yet they have been proven to be easy paths to prompt a mindset-shift.

Like with most changes, awareness is the first step – both awareness of the 12 Sustainability Principles listed above and awareness of one's own beliefs and behaviors in relation to these Principles. There are many resources available to learn how to develop a sustainability mindset, from rich literature to the Sustainability Mindset Indicator (SMI), a personal development tool to map and profile where an individual is on their journey towards a sustainability mindset. The SMI provides a personalized report with suggestions and questions to ponder (smindicator.com). It is also a tool for coaches and leadership development professionals, providing them with a picture of the team and suggestions of focused interventions.

Other resources include Resource Workbooks for educators, coaches, HR Business Partners, Learning and Development and Organization Development professionals, and corporate trainers, with exercises to specifically develop different aspects of the mindset, and specific sustainability mindset training and certifications.

So what are the implications and opportunities for leaders, coaches, teams and organizations?

I have titled this chapter "Sustainability — A Strategic Priority". This title has been chosen for a good reason. While previous sections of this book differentiated sustainability of the planet and of the organization, this is an operational distinction, to enable deepening the analysis of each, and by no means suggests there is a choice here. This is not to say that we don't hear every day some business people who make the firm their priority and postpone or disregard the sustainability of the planet. However, considering the sustainability of the planet as optional is myopic. To begin with, the planet encompasses the social and environmental aspects, not just the geological or climate related factors (which nevertheless are not minor). If we understand that planet means the whole ecosystem on which we live, and nature the only source of every single product we invent and use, we may get closer to understanding the relevance of 'the planet'. If we are not intentionally working for the planet, we are ultimately acting *against* it, because we continue contributing to the problems as opposed to making our daily decisions part of the solution-seeking. Furthermore, working against the planet means going against our own interest, as shareholders, stakeholders, employees, and as individuals. We are all in this together, and there is no Planet-B.

In the previous chapter it was highlighted how the Shared Leadership Disciplines® are instrumental to the sustainability of the firm. In our VUCA times, SLD® are the strategic option to navigate the challenging uncertain markets and circumstances.

The understanding of the sustainability of the whole is not optional. It is a strategic priority, because it becomes a strategic liability if unattended. Given the complexity of the challenges, combined with the urgency, the SLDs are a helpful life raft in this storm.

Further, SLDs are instrumental to the sustainability of the planet, which is being impacted by every single daily decision, whether intentional or not. The understanding of the sustainability of the whole is not optional. It is a strategic priority, because it becomes a strategic liability if unattended. Given the complexity of the challenges, combined with the urgency, the SLDs are a helpful life raft in this storm.

Therefore, every leader, team, coach and every organization has both an opportunity and a responsibility to ask the following questions:

1. What will I do to better understand my own mindset?
2. What aspects of a sustainability mindset do I need to further develop?
3. With whom do I need to **connect** in order to be an instrument for change in this area?

4. What **contract** (agreement) do I need with each of these stakeholders?
5. How will I **collect** their thoughts, feelings and wisdom to ensure their voices are heard?
6. How will we **collaborate** and work together to plan and then make measurable differences?
7. How will we **challenge** the status quo so we are constantly learning and growing?
8. What will we do as a team to be and work more sustainably from both perspectives of sustainability?
9. What will we do as organizations and businesses to work *for* our planet?
10. How will we improve our business by partnering with our planet?

By asking and getting answers to these questions we will stimulate a new way of thinking that will lead to changed behavior and a Sustainability Mindset both as leaders and coaches. Here's a question for all of us: ***"What will I do?"***

References:

[1] Rimanoczy, I. B. (2010). *Business leaders committing to and fostering sustainability initiatives.* Teachers College, Columbia University.

[2] Rimanoczy, I. (2017). *Big bang being: Developing the sustainability mindset.* Routledge.

[3] Ivanova, E., & Rimanoczy, I. (Eds.). (2021). *Revolutionizing Sustainability Education: Stories and Tools of Mindset Transformation.* Routledge.

[4] Rimanoczy, I. (2020). *The sustainability mindset principles: A guide to develop a mindset for a better world.* Routledge.

[5] Kassel & Rimanoczy (Eds.). Developing a Sustainability mindset in management education, 2016; Ritz & Rimanoczy (Eds.), Transformative leadership and sustainability mindset, 2021; Hermes, & Rimanoczy. (2018). *Deep learning for a sustainability mindset. The International Journal of Management Education, 16*(3), 460-467; SMI Resource Workbook Series, for Educators, Coaches and Consultants (2022).

[6] Rimanoczy, I. The Resource Workbook for Coaches. 2022

Part 4

Taking The Next Step

Becoming A Shared Leadership Team Coach

"Team coaching is partnering with a team leader and its members to co-create and achieve higher performance, with interdependence, self-sufficiency and learning as key outcomes."

The Authors

Most organizations are familiar with the concept of coaching. In fact, it is now commonplace for leaders and organizations to emphasize the importance of coaching and the benefits that a coaching culture brings.

In a 2019 study conducted by the International Coaching Federation (ICF) and the Human Capital Institute (HCI), among organizations with a strong coaching culture, 54% were classified as high-performing organizations, while among organizations without a strong coaching culture, only 29% were classified as high-performing organizations. In this study, indicators of a high-performing organization included senior leadership bench strength, high-performer retention and employer brand attraction.

The demand for trained coaches to support individuals and teams at all levels will continue to grow. These coaches can include leaders themselves who wear the coaching hat, in addition to the other hats that they wear in their work. There are also people who serve their clients as professional coaches, facilitators and consultants.

This chapter will focus on "Team Coaching" which concentrates on the skills and requirements of a Team Coach, which are more complex and varied than those used in coaching individuals. Team coaching is more intricate. It involves a range of interpersonal dynamics, different personalities, diverging work priorities and varied abilities. There are also different needs and wants. Team coaching is a relatively new area for many leaders and coaches. Even ICF announced its first formal set of team coaching competencies only in late 2020. We in LIM welcome this formalization of competencies as it helps in the development and raising of standards of team coaches. On our part, we will continue to contribute to the industry with our more than 35 years coaching teams around the globe.

The "interdependence", "self-sufficiency" and "learning" outcomes are key to the future sustainability of the team.

We define Team Coaching as ***a process of partnering with a team leader and its members to co-create and achieve higher performance, with interdependence, self-sufficiency and learning as key outcomes.*** The "interdependence", "self-sufficiency" and "learning" outcomes are key to the future sustainability of the team. In team coaching, not only do you want to help the team to perform better, but you also want the team to continue to support each other as well as continuing to use and learn from the tools that they have acquired. The net result is growth in the capability and capacity of the team and the individual members. Team coaching involves the science, art and tools to help the team to be greater than its individual members. ICF sees a Team Coach as someone who partners with a team in a co-creative and reflective process, taking into consideration the team dynamics and relationships, to inspire the team to reach its common purpose and shared goals.

No team comes to us ready-made. We have to make them ready.

Why is coaching essential for every team? At its core, a team is formed to achieve specific purposes and outcomes. This is its raison d'être. We must remember: ***No team comes to us ready-made. We have to make them ready.*** This means the team has to be molded, shaped and coached to maximize its performance and potential. Every team has untapped potential to raise its performance to the next level. Therefore, every team can benefit from team coaching, whatever its starting point.

Directive and less directive means

As a Team Coach, you will use a combination of both directive and less directive means when coaching a team. You are moving along a continuum with one mean at each end:

1. More directive

- You use more directive means when the team will benefit from your prescriptions and direct inputs such as learning new information or a new tool. You can also use this approach when the members have exhausted their own thinking and have run out of ideas. Generally, when team members do not know what they do not know, being more directive will be helpful to enable the team to move forward.

2. Less directive

- Using less directive means will give team members more space and latitude to develop their own insights, solutions and actions. This is preferred as you are engaging, empowering and enabling the members to experience and develop their own learning insights and answers. When you are less directive, you are giving opportunities not only for the members to think, but very importantly to let them own their solutions. With higher ownership comes higher commitment and accountability.

Although you will often shift between the two when working with a team, 70% to 80% of the time should be towards the less directive. Nothing is more powerful than empowering the team members to take 100% responsibility for their own solutions and decisions.

Your role and the different team coaching engagement approaches

Your role as a Team Coach is to partner and support the team to achieve its purpose and goals, and to be more effective. When engaging and coaching a team, you will adopt different approaches to engage the team. This depends on the team's needs, conditions and situations. A good parallel is that of a school teacher. In fulfilling the teacher's role, a teacher will use different methods such as teaching, discussion, experiments, readings, movies, team projects and field trips to create optimum learning moments for the learners.

Nothing is more powerful than empowering the team members to take 100% responsibility for their own solutions and decisions.

In the same vein, during a team coaching session, a Team Coach will use a combination of some, or all, of the below 5 approaches to engage the team (see Figure 16-1).

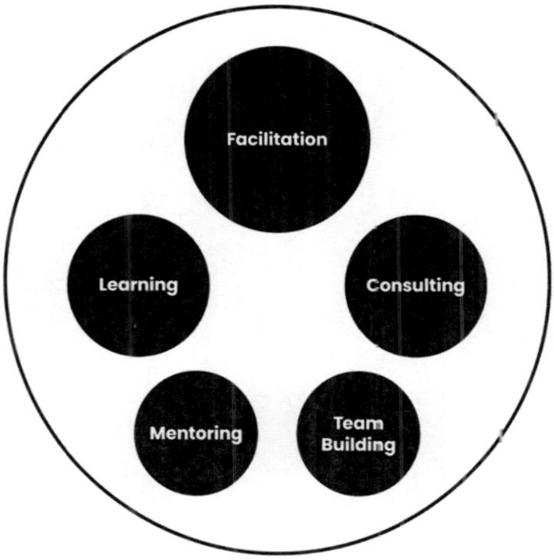

Figure 16-1: The Different Team Coaching Engagement Approaches

1. Team facilitation

A Team Coach facilitates open discussions by creating a safe and conducive environment for members to operate in. In this role, you will draw on a wide range of facilitation skills, tools and activities to enable every voice, thought, idea and feeling to be expressed and heard as each team strives for higher performance. Often, the discussions center around the goals and desired outcomes and what are needed to achieve them. During the facilitation, one of your key tasks is to evoke the awareness of the members to the different perspectives or views such as:

- From the past
- From the present
- From the future
- From a high level or strategic view
- From a wide-angle or lateral view
- From the short-, medium- and long-term view
- From the various stakeholders

Using the iceberg metaphor, you help the team to be aware of the entire iceberg, paying attention to the visible surface (their behaviors and actions) as well as the submerged portion that is driving what is on the surface. You are ready to help the team to address hidden dynamics and issues, including resolving misalignment, disengagement or any dysfunctions.

2. Team building

As a Team Coach, you will also design and use team building activities for experiential learning. Such activities form an essential part of your tool kit as adults learn from their experiences and reflections and they enjoy the opportunities to engage in problem-oriented activities. The Team Coach helps them to relate and connect their experiences from the activities to their own context, making the learnings relevant, real and immediately useable. Activities engage the body, appeal to the kinesthetic learners, provide fun and allow members to see each other in a different light.

3. Team learning (teaching)

In team coaching, you will also assume the role of a teacher, imparting knowledge, skills and tools to the team. Sharing knowledge or skills is important as the aim is to equip the team with the tools that will enable them to meet their immediate needs. The new tool will also help them to be better equipped to solve similar situations in the future. The "sharing" is kept brief and to the point. While it is usually integrated as part of your team coaching design, there are many opportunities during the session for you to seize the moment and impart a new learning. These Just-In-Time opportunities are powerful team coaching learning moments just when they need them.

4. Team mentoring

Using this approach, you will guide the team by sharing your own experiences. You will let the team learn from your personal stories, both the successful experiences as well as the failures that you have encountered in leading teams. You may also use your experience to act as the reflector and sounding board as the team explores its challenges and options. Team mentoring is usually kept to the essential moments as you do not want to do too much talking during a team coaching session. Share your experience only when needed or when asked. Let the team members have more airtime.

5. Team consulting

There are times in team coaching where you will provide your expert opinions and recommendations. A large part of the consulting process happens before the actual intervention begins. This includes collecting and analyzing data, discovering opportunities and gaps, and co-creating an appropriate design with the team. During the team coaching session, there are occasions when your expertise is needed or requested by the team. They will ask you for your "expert" recommendations or advice. In the same vein as mentoring, you should share your consulting thoughts only when needed. Your telling will not enable them to own the answers. Only they will own their own answers. In short, control yourself and do not rob the team of its own learning.

In essence, a Team Coach will use some or all the 5 approaches. How much time each will take will depend on the purpose, context and outcomes as well as the "who" you are working with. Before the session, the Consulting mode is key since discovery and diagnosis are needed to create an effective design that will determine how the team coaching session will flow, from start to end.

During the session, Team Facilitation, combined with Team Learning and Team Building, are frequently used to actively engage, equip and empower the participants. Mentoring and Consulting come to the fore only when required.

An effective Team Coach comes prepared with a well-thought-out design. On the other hand, the coach is ever ready to navigate and flow with the situation as it unfolds. A new insight, unexpected occurrence, surprise statement made, or unanticipated action taken, might lead to adjusting the plan on the spot. As one of our coaches often says: "The terrain is different from the map". What is important is the Team Coach stands ready with the skills, tools and judgment to be fully in service of the client.

Core skills of a Team Coach

When coaching a team, the Team Coach must be 100% present with a keen sense of observation and is ever ready to take whatever appropriate action is needed to support the team. This ability can be broken down into the following 6 core skills:

	Core skills of a Team Coach	Applications
1	Designing & Organizing	Before conducting the team coaching session, you will seek information from the client and discover what the client wants and needs. Collecting and diagnosing this information will enable you to design an appropriate solution for the client's approval. Once approved, you will use your organizing skills to plan, coordinate, prepare and ensure all the key elements are in place for the implementation. Elements will include the venue set-up, the preparation of the coaches, materials and other program details and logistics.
2	Presence & Listening	Presence and listening are two of the most critical skills needed in coaching. Your ability to be and to stay present with the team, listening to, and observing the team's situation, dynamics, personalities, abilities, attitudes and actions will help you to have the clarity and insights on what the team needs. The appropriate actions to take may include hitting the "pause" button for learning reflections, just-in-time learning of a tool to unlock their challenge or to even make real-time changes to your original session design.

Core skills of a Team Coach		Applications
3	Facilitating & Questioning	You will create psychological safety by setting up an environment that encourages openness, connectedness, caring, curiosity, courage, collaboration, commitment and learning. You will ask powerful coaching questions to facilitate reflection, discussion, freedom of expression as well as hearing all the voices and hearts in the room. You will also be adept at using experiential activities to create powerful learning moments and energy.
4	Communicating & Motivating	The ability to communicate concepts, processes and key information in an easy-to-understand manner is an essential skill to have. When you communicate well, the members will be more likely to accept, remember and apply what they have learned. You will also need to be good in motivating and inspiring the team leader and members to go beyond their comfort zone. An effective team coaching session will enable change and improvements to be realized.
5	Evaluating & Feedback	You will be skillful in providing timely evaluation and feedback that raise the awareness and enable the team to act on the feedback. Being fully present, alert and courageous will help you to select, pick and reflect back the visual, verbal and vocal messages and dynamics that the team has exhibited. Such observations and feedback can be powerful ways to evoke greater awareness for the team.
6	Challenging & Learning	As a Team Coach, you will challenge the team to push its "boundary" and be better than what it currently is, challenging the team at the personal, professional, team, organizational, business and the sustainability dimensions. You will seize and use every opportunity as Just-In-Time learning moments for the team and the individual members. You will role-model by being a keen learner yourself, curious to acquire new learning and being open to be challenged by the team that you are coaching.

Table 16-1: Core skills of a Team Coach

The necessary qualities of a Team Coach

An effective Team Coach possesses the below 5 qualities that every aspiring coach, with diligence and perseverance, can acquire:

1. Competence

- An effective Team Coach is competent and grounded in the science, art and tools of team coaching. By science is meant the ability to use andragogy to accelerate the learning of the adult learners. In LIM, our Shared Leadership Team Coaches actively apply the 10 Action Reflection Learning® principles with strong learning impact, regardless of industry or geography. The art of team coaching comes from applying wisdom and judgement to the actual practice, be it deliberately designing a solution, or just in time when the client needs it at that moment. There is no short cut to competence. The Team Coach also takes seriously the need to sharpen his or her saw to meet present and future needs. Key commitments include participating regularly in reflective coaching supervision, mentoring and community of practice. This keen desire to develop oneself continually is itself powerful role modeling.

2. Confidence

- The Team Coach is self-confident and exudes that confidence to the client. Confidence comes from competence. And equally important, it also comes from good preparation. A competent, well-prepared and grounded Team Coach will be confident to work with a client on any of their challenges. Confidence is also derived from having in hand a set of well-proven and tested team coaching tools. There are many situations where the Team Coach is using the tool for the first time with an actual client. Knowing the tool has been successfully used by other fellow coaches will boost the confidence of the Team Coach to use it. Confidence is an important quality as it adds to the trust that the client has in the coach.

3. Credibility

- Credibility is displayed when the Team Coach demonstrates mastery of the team coaching tools to the client and is able to help the client to experience and appreciate how the tools can help them to increase their team effectiveness. Credibility continues to be gained when the client notices small improvements and changes during and after the session. More solid credibility is obtained from your real practical experiences working with clients, including helping them achieve the qualitative and quantitative results, outcomes and returns that they are looking for. Doing practical team coaching work for clients is not easy to come by as many clients are reluctant to hire inexperienced coaches. One strategy for new coaches is to look for your friends and networks. Many will give you the chance, especially when you have developed good relationships with them. Another strategy is to be plugged into a community of team coaches where you can partner and collaborate with other experienced coaches in joint assignments.

4. Curiosity

- The attitude of curiosity will keep your mind, heart and all your senses open as you ask questions, explore and probe out of curiosity. This attitude is valuable to both your client and yourself. Because you assume nothing, your curiosity will enable un-asked questions to be asked and in the process, enable the team to break new ground.

5. Courage

- This is another valuable quality of a Team Coach — the courage to speak up, especially in areas that the client does not want to explore, but in fact needs to hear. It takes courage to challenge our clients, especially in a team setting. The Team Coach must be bold enough to lead the client to the uncomfortable zone and enable them to try new things and gain new experiences, learning and capabilities.

Undergirding these 5 qualities is the quality of authenticity. A Team Coach who is genuine, sincere and grounded will be able to develop trust with the leader and team, often within the first few minutes of interaction. A Team Coach who is not demonstrating authenticity and tries too hard to project what he or she is not, will face challenges at every stage of the team coaching process due to the trust deficit.

Our purpose as Team Coaches

As you read this and the earlier chapters, you can tell that the purpose, mission and impact of being a Team Coach can be of tremendous satisfaction to the Team Coach himself or herself. It goes beyond helping the clients to be higher performing. It is also helping them to be self-sufficient, self-sustaining and able to continue to learn and grow on their own, without you.

Our job should be to work ourselves out of the job! It is the best gift that you can give to them — that the team leader and team members have the ability to self-renew and self-generate independently. Metaphorically speaking, you have impacted their heads, hearts, hands and health in very positive and permanent ways. Thriving teams will help create thriving organizations. Employees in thriving organizations will return to their homes and children happier and more satisfied. This in turn will produce a thriving younger generation and a better society. Our Shared Leadership coaches are motivated by this sense of shared purpose which is our contribution towards building a better world for this and future generations.

Becoming a Shared Leadership Team Coach

The most effective way to be a Shared Leadership Team Coach is to learn from others. As Isaac Newton once said, we can look further by standing on the shoulders of giants. We have learned from giants in team coaching and hope to help others look further as well.

The ***Shared Leadership Team Coaching Academy***, the education arm of LIM, conducts team coaching programs for leaders, aspiring coaches as well as credentialed coaches who want to learn the Science, Tools, Art and the Real world (STAR) of team coaching. It is also relevant for trainers, facilitators and consultants looking for new skills and tools.

SHARED LEADERSHIP
TEAM COACHING ACADEMY

The ***Team Coach Certification Program (TCCP®)***, an approved ICF Level 1 program by the International Coaching Federation (ICF), develops coaches to be competent and confident working with teams using Shared Leadership and Action Reflection Learning (ARL®) principles, processes and tools. The purpose of the TCCP® is to enable more versatile Shared Leadership Team Coaches who can partner and empower individuals and teams to become even more effective, thereby creating & sustaining a better world.

The TCCP® is the go-to program for:

1. New and aspiring coaches

You will start with the basics and progressively become competent in coaching teams and individuals. The TCCP® will enable you to attain the ICF Level 1 certificate, which is a pre-requisite for your ICF Associate Certified Coach (ACC) credential.

2. Experienced coaches

You will learn the ropes and skills required for team coaching. This is a practical course where you gain team coaching knowledge and tools, and applying them with a real client as part of your practical work. The TCCP® will also help you to meet one of the key requirements for the ICF Advanced Certification In Team Coaching (ACTC) credentials.

3. Leaders and internal coaches

Leaders and internal coaches can learn team coaching skills through a tailored in-company TCCP®. This allows several leaders within the same organization to be developed and equipped with the same coaching philosophy and tool kit.

To learn more, you can visit: https://www.limglobal.net/learning

Community of Practice

During the program, you will learn with the Academy's staff coaches and your peers. You will practice your skills for real-world applications. As a graduate, you can continue your learning and networking in the Academy's Shared Leadership Coaching Community of Practice and the various learning activities. In the Academy, we believe in connecting, learning and collaborating together, even after the formal classes. As our community grows, so will our contributions to the world of leadership, coaching and sustainability.

SHARED LEADERSHIP COACHING
Community of Practice

Connect. Learn. Collaborate.

So What? …… Insights

The impact of shared leadership team coaching is far-reaching. A well-coached shared leadership team brings about immense benefits that include:

- The team is well motivated, well-oiled and well on track to achieving and maximizing its purpose and potential.
- Every member in the team is willing and ready to speak and step up and to take on more ownership and leadership
- Enjoying a higher performing team culture that provides sustainable results
- Experiencing a higher quality of work life as the team has better capability and capacity to meet expectations, and enjoy working with each other in the team
- Creating happier and more sustainable families, homes and ultimately, a better world

This is the reason why becoming a Shared Leadership Team Coach can be so meaningful and inspiring. You are encouraging and enabling leaders to share more of their Influence, Power and Ownership with their people. This empowers team members the freedom and space to speak up, step up and take on more leadership with even greater sense of purpose.

As you work with one team at a time, you will never exactly know the ripple effect of your work. You never know how far the ripples will go or for how long the ripples will continue. But one thing is certain. It starts with you as the Team Coach who is willing to take the first step to start the ripples. Just one team at a time. For a better world.

"One team at a time. For a better world"

Afterword
by Willie Andersen

As you complete reading this book, one question that many of you may have is, "How do I create a shared leadership culture within my team?" That is a familiar question, and the answer is not as challenging as you may think. I have found that once you get to a place where you truly want a "shared leadership culture," the rest is easy. You will know if you "truly want" a shared leadership culture by how easy or difficult it is for you to "let go" of whatever control you currently have in your team.

To do this, as a first step, my advice is to simply ask your team for help. Yes, just tell your team that you need their help in co-creating a shared leadership culture within your team and across your company. Explain why it's important to you and them. By asking for their help, you are modeling the first important step of sharing leadership. They will respond in a very positive way. Next, cite a real challenge that you and your team are facing. When facing a challenge, team members tend to feel that "we are all in this together" and that begins to answer some of the other "C's of the 5 SLDs."

Most challenges present themselves as undesirable situations. Invite your team to make the situation less undesirable or perhaps even favorable. An ideal challenge is one where there is no recognized expert on the team. If you have someone who positions himself as the "expert," then others will feel less likely to contribute or share leadership. Often everyone looks to the team leader, as it is a typical expectation that the leader will "lead" by default. Just avoid the temptation to "feel the obligation to lead." Ask others to share their good ideas. Ensure that everyone's voice is heard. When everyone on the team has a similar understanding of the challenge, shared leadership will surface. The Challenge will position the team to begin the journey in moving towards a Shared Leadership culture.

When there is a shared challenge, you will notice that team members begin to organize themselves and quickly identify roles, rules and seek clarification – Collect, Collaborate and Connect. They also will want to learn more about the challenge - What does success look like? – Define and Align (Contract).

If you are the team leader, select one of the many challenges you face today. Instead of feeling a need to go through all the C's in sequential order, start with the Challenge and be aware of the other C's so that they all get the proper attention. This book has equipped you with the tools to bring each of the 5 Cs to life.

Just get started. The first step will lead to the second. You will quickly be on your way. Enjoy the journey. And even more, enjoy the company – you and your team. You will soon be saying, ***'Thank God it's Today.'***

Appendix 1:
Summary of Shared Leadership Disciplines® and ARL® Tools

Definition: Shared leadership is a leadership approach where leaders give more influence, power and ownership (IPO) to their team members, enabling them to speak up, step up and take on more leadership and ownership, with a higher sense of purpose.

<table>
<tr><th colspan="2">Shared Leadership Disciplines®</th><th>What it means</th><th>Action Reflection Learning® Principles</th><th>Some of the Action Reflection Learning® tools highlighted in this book</th></tr>
<tr><td>1</td><td>Connect</td><td>The discipline of Connect is to engage, understand and care for each other at the personal and professional levels. It is also feeling “connected” with the team, organization and the business. To connect is to appreciate, relate and empathize.</td><td rowspan="5">Principle 1: Tacit Knowledge

Principle 2 : Relevance

Principle 3: Reflection

Principle 4: Self-Awareness

Principle 5: Integral

Principle 6: Social Learning

Principle 7: Systems Thinking

Principle 8: Facilitated Learning

Principle 9: Paradigm Shift

Principle 10: Repetition and Reinforcement</td><td rowspan="5">• Check-in (Chap 4)
• Extended coffee breaks (Chap 4)
• Walk & Talk (Chap 4)
• Stories (Chap 4)
• MyStory (Chap 4)
• OurStory (Chap 4)
• Memorable Moments (Chap 4)
• “Catch of the Day” (Chap 4)
• Norms Setting
• Team / Leader Contracting (Chap 5)
• Role Contracting (Chap 5)
• Stop Reflect Write Report - SRWR (Chap 6)
• Reflection & Dialogue (Chap 6)
• Gallery Walk (Chap 6)
• Surveys and 1:1 conversations (Chap 6)
• 4MAT (Chap 9)
• Meeting Management (Chap 7)
• Peer Learning Process - PLP (Chap 7)
• Fish Bowl (Chap 7)
• Power Planning Process (Chap 7)
• Check-up (Chap 7)
• Personal Passion Project (Chap 8)
• Pentagon-Plus System Model (Chap 5 & 12)</td></tr>
<tr><td>2</td><td>Contract</td><td>The discipline of Contract is getting alignment, agreement and commitment around expectations of work and relationships, now and the future. To contract is to commit and gain accountability.</td></tr>
<tr><td>3</td><td>Collect</td><td>The discipline of Collect is to proactively seek the facts, thoughts, feelings, energy as well as the collective wisdom and intelligence, from both within the team as well as from outside it. To collect is to be curious and complete.</td></tr>
<tr><td>4</td><td>Collaborate</td><td>The discipline of Collaborate is about working together towards common goals. It combines the science of planning and the art of cooperation. To collaborate is to invite and co-create.</td></tr>
<tr><td>5</td><td>Challenge</td><td>The discipline of Challenge is to constantly question the status quo, pushing the envelope, encouraging new thinking, so as to get and stay ahead. To challenge is to be open and to change.</td></tr>
</table>

Appendix 2:
30 Check-In Questions For More Engaging Connections

What is Check-In?

Check-in is an activity to allow team or group members the opportunity to share or disclose a little more of themselves at the personal level in a light and easy way. Check-in is usually conducted at the start of any meeting or team coaching session.

Why is it useful?

This is useful as it is a quick way to build rapport, thus creating a more relaxed and personalized atmosphere to begin a session. By doing so, you will enable every voice to be heard right from the start. When you are able to engage every individual in the room in the first few minutes, you will have a higher chance that they will be engaged with you for the rest of the session. As check-in is a safe space to allow personal sharing, over time, there is a deepening of inter-personal trust and understanding between and among you and your team members.

How is it done?

This is fairly simple. Think of a question that allows everyone to share. Give everyone 30 seconds to think and collect their thoughts. When everyone is ready, let everyone take turns to share. It is a good practice to let everyone know how much sharing time they have. A good sharing can be completed within 30 to 60 seconds. Depending on the group size, this process can be completed within 5 to 10 minutes. If you make check-in a routine in your meetings, you can invite a different member in your team to come up with a "Check-In" question for each team meeting.

What are some of our favorite check-in questions?

Listed below are some of the favorite questions that we use at our meetings and team coaching sessions in LIM. Many of these questions come from our Shared Leadership Coaches. Try them out, add your own questions or adapt these questions. Compile your own list of interesting check-in questions.

1. What makes me smile?
2. What's 'new or news' outside of my work?
3. What is one good thing that has happened to me at the personal level in the last few weeks?
4. What is something I am grateful for recently?
5. What outdoor activities or pastimes do I enjoy?
6. What is my favorite drink (or food, color, animal, holiday destination etc.) and why?
7. What am I looking forward to in the upcoming week (or weekend)?
8. What is my Zen moment and where do I find it?

9. How do I normally unwind after work? Over the weekend?
10. What is one non-work activity that I tried recently?
11. What is one activity or subject that I am keen to learn but have not yet started?
12. What's something most people don't know about me?
13. What is one image or phrase that inspires me?
14. When am I most creative?
15. What helps me perform at my best?
16. What is one of my favorite sayings, slogans or quotes and why?
17. What is one dish I might prepare for the team someday?
18. How would I like to celebrate my next birthday?
19. What kind of place would I most like to visit, and why?
20. What is one "thing" that I want to add into my personal life?
21. What is my number one personal goal for the next six months?
22. What is my most prized physical possession?
23. What is one achievement, outside work, that makes me proud?
24. When I was young, what did I want to be when I grew up?
25. Who is one family member or friend whom I admire and why?
26. If I could display a single photograph of my life, what would it show?
27. What is a fond childhood memory that I have?
28. If I could go back in time and give advice to a younger version of yourself, what advice would I give?
29. What book has had the greatest influence on my life and why?
30. What's the best (worst) decision I've ever made?

So what as a result of using check-ins?

Little drops of water makes the mighty ocean. These words of wisdom aptly apply to the check-in activity. The 5 to 10 minutes that you invest in a check-in helps build an ocean of trust, relationships and connectedness in the team. High intentionality and consistency are key. Check-in helps make the workplace more fun, warm and human. "Thank God it's today!"

Appendix 3:
Our Top 15 Frequently Asked Questions

We have received many questions over the years from participants in our programs, workshops and webinars about ***Shared Leadership Disciplines*** and ***Team Coaching.*** We have selected 15 that we believe might be of interest to our readers.

Shared Leadership Disciplines

1. Why is Shared Leadership powerful in both Executive and Team coaching?

As executive coaches and team coaches we frequently have opportunities to coach team leaders. Many of their concerns revolve around this question: "How can I be a more effective leader and get the best out of my team?" Once people understand what Shared Leadership Disciplines are, they will be in a better position to ask the leaders questions relating to each of the five disciplines, and to help them discover what they are doing now that is working, and what they might consider changing. Our knowledge and ability to ask effective open questions, and where appropriate, offer them relevant Shared Leadership frameworks and tools, will enable our clients to move from this focus question to concrete changes which they themselves will define and commit to do.

2. How can we as coaches support leadership sharing in our client systems?

First, we must understand, and always practice it ourselves.

Second, we can encourage conversations around four related questions: **What** is it? **Why** is it such a powerful leadership style? **How** does it work? **So what** can we do to adopt, adapt and apply the disciplines and bring them to life in our own teams and organizations?

Third, we can support senior leaders to adopt and model shared leadership behaviors.

Fourth, we can encourage them to cascade these disciplines and tools to their own teams.

Fifth, we can offer our support as coaches to make that happen. Therefore, we are supporting a major organizational paradigm shift that will benefit any company. anywhere, to heighten engagement, improve performance and increase profitability.

3. How does LIM's flock of geese logo relate to Shared Leadership?

When geese fly together, they can travel 70% further than they can flying alone. When geese fly as a flock – or a gaggle — and arrange themselves in formation behind the leader, they get a little extra lift and don't have to spend as much energy to maintain altitude and forward momentum. The less they flap, the more energy they conserve, and the further the whole flock can fly. The lead goose lessens the wind resistance on those behind him, so they rotate positions in the flock as they fly so no one goose is always flying in the lead role or at the back. Additionally, they have been observed supporting those geese who get sick; they look after one another. This struck us as an important metaphor for the effective sharing of leadership.

4. How can a leader act as both leader and coach to a team?

We are living in a period when leaders are expected to do more, better, and faster, with fewer resources and less time. Teams cannot always afford to have a coach with them, so, today's successful team leaders increasingly wear the hat of both leader and coach. Together, these roles represent a formidable challenge because they involve a wide range of responsibilities, and differing skill sets. Further, each 'hat' has a different look, is worn in differing situations, serves a separate purpose, and the leader must be clear about the responsibilities of each. Perhaps one way to view the two roles is to accept that developing team members is the overall responsibility of the leader. As he does this, he pays attention to his operational responsibilities and to his professional development responsibilities. Both are valuable in helping him to prepare new leaders for the organization.

In the operational realm, the main responsibilities include: preparing for meetings; facilitating meetings; ensuring effective decision-making; debriefing meetings; checking in; ensuring observation of the team norms; updating late-comers to meetings; managing time; documenting decisions and next steps; following up on commitments. In Shared Leadership these tasks and responsibilities can, and indeed should, be shared and delegated. Not only does the act of sharing lessen the burden on the team leader, but it helps the leader by giving him time to plan and strategize. This gives team members the chance to gain the skills they will need to become the next generation of leaders. A Win/Win. Note: There may be some responsibilities a team leader is unable to delegate.

5. How do we help authoritative leaders embark on a Shared Leadership journey?

What we can do is to clearly articulate what Shared Leadership is – how it can help any leader become more effective by sharing responsibility, by being open to new ways of leading, and by asking for help. Most leaders are looking for profitability and higher performance from their team, and to achieve this, many still believe that to do so they must become more demanding of the team.

Most authoritative or directive leaders ignore the power in listening with empathy, of inquiry, of telling stories and creating a psychologically safe environment where everyone can say what he thinks and feels. They mistakenly feel that they 'should have the answers', and that to ask for help is a sign of weakness. To encourage them, we invite them to reflect on their own experiences, and to recall when they were at their best, and to rediscover what they did, how they behaved, how they thought. We find that in their recollections, they discover they exhibited some, if not all the SL disciplines! Once they are aware of sustainable behaviors that really work, they will be ready to take a few small steps that can dramatically change their leadership behavior. Feedback and reflection are the best catalysts for change. We have seen many 'authoritative leaders' change by seeking and responding to feedback from their team. Awareness is a first step to transformation. Be patient and persistent.

6. How can Shared Leadership help any team become more engaged, effective and happier?

All work involves pressure. Enlightened teams can identify how to mitigate restrictive and avoidable stress factors by sharing leadership, having the freedom to speak up and be heard without judgment. This reduces stress and ultimately makes life at work more engaging and productive. Significant by-products are more ideas, better decisions, higher performance, greater profitability, and greater happiness.

Team Coaching

7. How different is team coaching from individual coaching, using the ICF competencies?

While the ICF competencies for team coaching and individual coaching are similar, there are clear variations in their application. The biggest difference between individual and team coaching is the 'complexity' inherent in dealing with a larger number of people in the session. Team members can range from three to as many as fifteen or more, compared to only one in individual coaching. Thus, the dynamics in coaching teams are much more complex, challenging, and exciting. The coach must attend to interpersonal undercurrents, to ensure that every voice is heard and respected, that decisions are inclusive, that next steps are clear, and the 5Cs are supported. This situation creates a need for competent and experienced Team Coaches who can calmly, confidently and competently manage this complexity.

8. What is the difference between Team Coaching and Team Facilitation?

Team coaching and team facilitation have the common aim of helping any team to become higher performing as one of the primary outcomes. However, what sets team coaching apart from team facilitation is that in team coaching, there is a consistent emphasis on enabling the leader and the team members to:

a. Think and work more interdependently among themselves, and with all their key stakeholders
b. Be more self-sufficient by being equipped with team coaching concepts, skills and tools that they can apply on their own without the presence of a coach
c. Continue to learn even as they work, ensuring their rate of learning is greater than, or equal to, the rate of change.

Team facilitators, on the other hand, usually do not emphasize interdependency, self-sufficiency and learning during or after their engagement. Their focus and remit is to help the team to achieve the pre-agreed objectives within the given timeframe. The attention of the facilitator is on the present engagement and not beyond. Team coaches, on the other hand, focus on the immediate team objectives and at the same time, consider what is best to sustain the performance and outcomes for the leader and the team after the engagement.

9. How can we increase our own effectiveness and efficiency as team coaches?

Here are three easy things we can do to increase our own effectiveness as team coaches:

a. Focus on our own self and our skills development
b. Continuously learn to know how we can master the 5 SLDs and seek to expand our team coaching tool kit.
c. Keep in good shape physically, psychologically, mentally, and spiritually.

Here are three things we can do to increase our own efficiency as team coaches.

1. Be prepared.
2. Practice; Practice; Practice.
3. Debrief every meeting so we know what is working and what needs to change.

As we do these activities, we become clearer in our own minds how critical it is for us to encourage our coaches do the same! Leading by example is the best way to lead.

10. What are six dimensions that team coaches should be prepared to support?

We believe there are six dimensions that team coaches can help teams to address:

a. **Personal:** Facilitate check-ins; storytelling; connecting constantly; increasing awareness; making sure everyone is included.
b. **Professional:** Peer learning; giving and receiving feedback; creating learning conversations.
c. **Team:** Setting norms; clarifying team/leader expectations; agreeing on meeting protocols; deciding how to take decisions.
d. **Organizational:** Agreeing upon organizational values and behaviors; clarifying roles and responsibilities.
e. **Business:** Defining purpose; clarifying a team's mission, vision, strategy and annual targets.
f. **Sustainability:** Examining the impact of the organization and team on the environment and society.

11. Why is it important to have a wide variety of tools in our tool kit?

Carpenters, plumbers, mechanics, doctors, dentists, etc. all need tools. Coaches too. And we need a wide variety to be able to use for the many different team needs we will be facing and for each of the 5 SLDs. We need to know how and when to use these tools to bring impact and health to our clients, their teams and their organizations. We need to constantly learn and grow to be better coaches ourselves. We get this 'skill' development along with 'mindset' development through coaching supervision, mentoring, experience, training, conferences, reading, writing and other development programs.

12. How can we collect what matters most to the teams?

Ask the team!

There are several ways to find out what's on the minds of the individuals in a team. Here are two that we use:

1. Invite them for a conversation (not an interview); an interview is more formal and can lead to defensiveness. Take time to introduce yourselves and then move into 'What's on your mind related to our upcoming workshop?' After taking time to connect in an informal conversation you have a better chance of hearing what they really think and feel.
2. Conduct a survey among members. We frequently ask all team members to send us one question that is on their mind before any intervention that they hope we address in our team workshop. We organize their questions into a survey, and send out the list of questions to the whole team. We stress that their answers will be anonymous but not confidential. That is, we gather all the replies in a document but we do not identify the author of any question. Then we share all survey comments with all team members just before our intervention (team workshop or meeting). This document is most helpful in alerting members, and us coaches, to the salient issues facing the team. Importantly, it can be instrumental in helping us to design the workshop.

13. What is the #1 challenge that team coaches face and what can they do?

Most challenges we have faced as team coaches relate to 'engagement' or the lack of 'engagement'. One of our jobs as coaches is to co-create a psychologically 'safe' environment with the team leader and with his team so everyone feels comfortable speaking their minds. Almost everyone wants to add value. We all want to be heard and appreciated. We as coaches have the tools to help teams effectively engage in every aspect of their work – connecting, contracting, collecting, collaborating, and challenging. We as coaches need to be equipped to help a team with every one of those activities. Perhaps the two easiest and best interventions we can make are: 1) helping teams Connect and 2) Contract. We have found that even with intact teams it is essential to establish good connections, and then to define a clear set of expectations between the team and team leader, and among each of the members.

14. How can Team Coaches create the right PLACE to increase employee engagement?

Employees will be more engaged when five key elements are found in the team. These elements will create the right P.L.A.C.E. that enable them to speak up, step up and take on more leadership and ownership in the team:

a. **P**urpose that is aligned on all six dimensions
b. **L**eadership that is shared, allowing everyone to speak up and share the ownership
c. **A**utonomy that gives people more control over their work and lives
d. **C**onnections that build personal understanding, relationships and trust
e. **E**ndowments (gifts) that each team member brings to the team — to use and to grow

15. How do I choose the right team coach certification program?

Look for a team coach certification program where you get proper development, familiarity with the variety and complexity of team dynamics while learning vital concepts and tools that are appropriate for each of the 5 Shared Leadership Disciplines – Connect; Contract; Collect; Collaborate; Challenge.

Make sure the program offers more than just good team theory. Make sure you get experiences where you can apply concepts and tools with real team clients. Ensure that the program you select also provides mentoring opportunities, so you have an experienced mentor coach to give you feedback and valuable tips.

After the certification, having an active community of practice with fellow coaches to continue sharpening and expanding your team coaching knowledge and skills will also be an essential criteria in your selection of a suitable certification program. It will even be better if the community is the right P.L.A.C.E. to network, have business collaborations, develop friendships and help make your team coaching journey purposeful, supported and fun.

Bibliography

Bartol, K.M. & Martin (1986). *Women and men in task groups.* New York, Academic Press.

Bass, B M (1960). *Leadership, Psychology and Organizational Behavior.* New York: Harper.

Betterup, *What is Self-Awareness.* https://www.betterup.com/blog/what-is-self-awareness

Boldren, Richard, *Distributed Leadership in Organizations: A Review of Theory and Research,* International Journal of Management Reviews 13, no. 3 (September 2011): 251–69.

Decoding Global Ways of Working. https://www.bcg.com/publications/2021/advantages-of-remote-work-flexibility

Galton, F (1869). *Hereditary Genius.* New York: Appleton.

Burke, C.S., Fiore, S.M. & Salas, E (2003) *The Role of Shared Cognition in Enabling Shared Leadership and Team Adaptability.* In Pearce, C.L. & Conger, J.A. Shared leadership: Reframing the hows and whys of leadership. London: Sage.

Cox, J., Pearce, C. & Perry, M. (2003) *Toward a model of shared leadership and distributed influence in the innovation process: How shared leadership can enhance new product development team dynamics and effectiveness. In C. Pearce & J. Conger (Eds.) Shared leadership.* Thousand Oaks, CA: Sage.

Craig L. Pearce and Jay A. Conger. (2003) *All Those Years Ago: The Historical Underpinnings of Shared Leadership. In Shared Leadership: Reframing the Hows and Whys of Leadership*, ed. Craig L. Pearce and Jay A. Conger. Thousand Oaks, CA: Sage.

Dachler, H. P., & Wilpert, B. (1978) *Conceptual dimensions and boundaries of participation in organizations: A critical evaluation.* Administrative Science Quarterly.

Daniel H. Pink. (2009) *Drive: The Surprising Truth about What Motivates Us. New York*: Riverhead Books.

Dansereau, F; Graen, G; Haga, W. J. (1975). *A Vertical Dyad linkage approach to leadership in formal organizations.*

Dumaine, B. (1994) *The trouble with teams.* Fortune, September 4 issue.

Fletcher, J. K. & Käufer, K. (2003). *Shared leadership: Paradox and possibility.* In Pearce, Craig L. & Conger, Jay A. (eds). *Shared leadership: Reframing the hows and whys of leadership.* London: Sage. P. 21-47.

Harvard Business Review, *Knowledge Workers Are More Productive From Home.* https://hbr.org/2020/08/research-knowledge-workers-are-more-productive-from-home

Harvard Business Review, *Kodak Downfall Wasn't About Technology.* https://hbr.org/2016/07/kodaks-downfall-wasnt-about-technology

Hooker, C. & Csikszentmihalyi, M. (2003). *Flow, Creativity, and Shared Leadership.* In Pearce, C.L. & Conger, J.A. (eds). *Shared leadership: Reframing the hows and whys of leadership.* London: Sage. P. 217-234.

John L. Cotton, David A. Vollrath, Kirk L. Froggatt, Mark L. Lengnick-Hall and Kenneth R. Jennings. *Employee Participation: Diverse Forms and Different Outcomes.*

King, Albert (1990). *Evolution of Leadership Theory*, Indian Council of Social Science Research Publications, Vol. 15, No. 2, April-June 1990

Knowles, Malcolm S, *The Modern Practice Of Adult Learning, From Pedagogy to Andragogy*. Revised and Updated. Cambridge Adult Education, Prentice Hal Regents, Englewood Cliffs, NJ 07632

Lashway, Larry (2003). *Distributed Leadership*. National Association of Elementary School Principals, Research Roundup; Volume 19, Number 4, Summer.

Locke, E. E. (2003) Good definitions: *The epistemological foundation of scientific progress*. In J. Greenberg (ED.) *Organizational behavior: The state of the science*. Mahwah, NJ: Erlbaum.

Manz, C.C., & Sims, H.P. Jr (1989). *SuperLeadership: Leading others to lead themselves*. New York: Prentice Hall

Manz, C C and Sims, H P, Jr. (1987). *Leading Workers to Lead Themselves: The External Leadership of Self-Managing Work Teams*. Administrative Science Quarterly, 32,106- 28.

Margaret Wheatley and Deborah Frieze, *Leadership in the Age of Complexity: From Hero to Host*. Resurgence & Ecologist 264 (January/February 2011 electronic).

Mckinsey, *It's time for leaders to get real about hybrid*. https://www.mckinsey.com/business-functions/people-and-organizational-performance/our-insights/its-time-for-leaders-to-get-real-about-hybrid?hdpid=fa5f295d-22d1-4d18-a368-6ce9d5d48c7f&hctky=12633921&hlkid=c8eef22316ce472382abfb65e6c71048

Monica Brinkerhoff, Albert Murrieta, and Cassandra O'Neill. *Collective Leadership: Activating the Gifts of Your Team*. Exchange (November/December 2015): 51–54.

Northouse, Peter. *Leadership: Theory and Practice*. Sage Publications, 2015

O'Toole, J., Galbraith, J., & Lawler, E. E. (2002), *When Two (or More) Heads are Better Than One: The Promises and the Pitfalls of Shared Leadership*, California Management Review 44(4): 65–83.

Pearce, C.L. and Sims, H.P. (2000), *Shared leadership: Toward a multi-level theory of leadership, Advances in Interdisciplinary Studies of Work Teams (Advances in Interdisciplinary Studies of Work Teams, Vol. 7)*, Emerald Group Publishing Limited, Bingley, pp. 115-139.

Pearce, C. & Conger, J. (2003) *All those years ago: The historical underpinnings of shared leadership.* In C. Pearce & J. Conger (Eds.) Shared leadership. Thousand Oaks, CA: Sage.

Positive Psychology, *Operant Conditioning Theory.* https://positivepsychology.com/operant-conditioning-theory/

Rimanoczy, Isabel and Ernie Turner. *Action Reflection Learning: Solving Real Business Problems By Connecting Learning With Earning.* Davies Black Publishing, 2008

Robert Half Research, http://rh-us.mediaroom.com/2020-11-23-Working-Weekends-a-Reality-for-Nearly-7-in-10-Remote-Professionals-Robert-Half-Research-Shows

Self-Awareness. A White Paper. https://www.insights.com/media/1744/self-awareness-white-paper.pdf

Shared Leadership. https://en.wikipedia.org/wiki/Shared_leadership

Swieringa, Joop and Andre Wierdsma. *Becoming A Learning Organisation: Beyond The Learning Curve.* Addison-Wesley Publishers, 1992

Tan, Swee Heng, *Coaching In The Moment, How Busy Leaders Can Make More Impact With Less Time*, Candid Creation Publishing LLP, 2017

The Cynefin Framework. https://www.godaddy.com/garage/cynefin-suggestive-framework-problem-solving/

Trollestad, C. (2003). Existentiellt välbefinnande & moralisk trovärdighet: hos högre chefer och ledare. (Translated: *Existential well-being and moral credibility: With senior executives and leaders*). Stockholm: Svenska förl.

Turner, Ernie, *Gentle Interventions For Team Coaching, Little Things That Make A Big Difference*, Leadership In Management LLC, 2013.

Vroom, V. H., & Jago, A. G. (1988). *The new leadership: Managing participation in organizations.* Prentice-Hall, Inc.

West, M., Lyubovnikova, J., Eckert, R. and Denis, J-L. (2014), *CL for cultures of high quality health care*, Journal of Organizational Effectiveness: People and Performance, Vol.1 Iss 3 pp. 240-260

Other Books By The Authors

About The Authors

Ernie Turner is the President of LIM (Leadership in Motion), a global consulting firm focused on development – people and business – simultaneously using LIM's 10 ARL® (Action Reflection Learning) principles. In this capacity, he has been building LIM as an international consulting firm over the last 36 years focused on Shared Leadership, learning, team coaching and developing team coaches.

Ernie has coached numerous executives and their leadership teams both virtually and face to face across 40 countries. Ernie has an ACC ICF credential. He has written numerous articles and books on leadership, teamwork, and team coaching including: "Action Reflection Learning: Solving Real Business Problems by Connecting Learning with Earning" co-authored with Isabel Rimanoczy, Ernie's life partner, "Gentle Interventions for Team Coaching: Little things that make a BIG difference" and "Shared Leadership Disciplines®: A Better way to lead and coach" co-authored with Tan Swee Heng, one of Ernie's business partners.

One of Ernie's passions is to create a more sustainable and peaceful world utilizing Shared Leadership Disciplines® and ARL® principles. Ernie's other interests include peer learning, large scale change, piano, tennis, scuba and golf. He is a frequent speaker and facilitator in webinars and conferences.

Tan Swee Heng helps leaders to share more of their leadership & bring out the best of themselves and their teams. He envisions we can have a better world with more thriving leaders and coaches at the workplace. This has been his life purpose since he embarked on his professional coaching journey in 2010.

Today, Swee Heng, as the Head of LIM's Shared Leadership Team Coaching Academy, dedicates his energy to developing coaches' effectiveness and well-being through coaching supervision and mentoring; imparting shared leadership team coaching skills in the Team Coach Certification Program® and coaching leaders and executives, from the C-Suite to team leads, to thrive and perform for sustainable outcomes.

Swee Heng is an International Coaching Federation's Master Certified Coach (MCC), a certified Coach Supervisor & Shared Leadership Team Coach. With his 31 years of prior practitioner experience working in 3 large organizations, Swee Heng deeply understands the hopes and challenges of leaders and teams, many of them needing support to be better at balancing organizational goals, stakeholders and their personal needs.

At home Swee Heng is blessed with his wife, Jean and his son and daughter, both of whom are Gen Z in their twenties: E-Liang and E-Zhen. Swee Heng enjoys reading, morning jogs and also loves to spend time in the kitchen to prepare nourishing meals for his family. His motto: Enjoy the moments!